PRAISE FOR
THE UNFURLING FROND

"With insight and skill, Rebecca Beardsall shows a reader the expansiveness that life can offer if you're willing to search for it. And Beardsall is an endless, relentless seeker. Part love letter to a former self, part love letter to a destined partnership, *The Unfurling Frond* feels most like a love letter to New Zealand, the country to which she moved in the late 1990s during the early boom of internet dating. Profoundly romantic yet rigorously self-examined, Beardsall's book shows us what it's like to be a believer, to so fully believe in one's life path even as it shifts and turns and surprises. Over the course of forty-plus years and across continents and oceans, Beardsall echoes the legendary Lebanese writer Etel Adnan, who wrote: 'I am always away from something and somewhere.' And yet Beardsall grounds us over and over again throughout her transformations, demonstrating that 'Home lives inside my body.'"

– Jefferson Navicky, author of
Head of Island Beautification for the Rural Oulands

"Rebecca Beardsall's *The Unfurling Frond* is such a joy to read! We enter this exploration of self through many doorways, each one offering us a new angle of vision. From a lush description of a fictional perfume called 'Rebecca' to smart reconsideration of *Alice in Wonderland*, Beardsall's voice beckons us to follow her through the spirals of time."

– Brenda Miller, author of
A Braided Heart: Essays on Writing and Form

"*The Unfurling Frond* is a thoughtful meditation on the spaces we inhabit, on how they define us and we define them. Following them from Colonial Pennsylvania to colonized New Zealand, Rebecca Beardsall beautifully explores moving between places, time, identity and personhood."

– Liz Prato, author of
Kids in America: A Gen X Reckoning

"A love story, a family memoir, a travel- and home-finding narrative: Rebecca Beardsall's *The Unfurling Frond* traverses genre to explore the multiple strands of her becoming. The spiraling koru frond is a central metaphor, its unfurling a way to understand movements across time and space, and Rebecca's own journey from a small town in Pennsylvania to an urban apartment in Auckland, New Zealand's largest city. Along the way, she finds meaning in the midst of great loss and hope in a great love. Inspiring, moving, and inventive, *The Unfurling Frond* is a joyous read."

– Kristiana Kahakauwila,
author of *This is Paradise: Stories*

THE UNFURLING FROND

A MEMOIR OF BELONGING AND BECOMING

REBECCA BEARDSALL

atmosphere press

© 2023 Rebecca Beardsall

Published by Atmosphere Press

Cover design by Kevin Stone

No part of this book may be reproduced without permission from the author except in brief quotations and in reviews. This is a work of fiction, and any resemblance to real places, persons, or events is entirely coincidental.

Atmospherepress.com

For Geoffrey

CONTENTS

Prologue: Blank Slate/White Bag ... 3

SECTION I

May 25, 1991	11
Vision to Venture	13
I Thee Wed..And With It I Bestow All of the Treasures	15
Rocking and Rolling	17
Becky	20
Beyond Becky	27
Undersea Cables	37
Echo of Myself	39
mIRC - Internet Relay Chat	42
Time Zones	46
Wedding Day	50
Heart of Steel	51
Ring of Fire	52
Pieces of Me	55
Climbing Branches	57
Everything Has Two Names	60
Regency Apartments, 4h/Lorne Street	62
Livewire	63
What Risk?	67
Byline	70
Husband	74
What Do You See?	75

Piha	84
That's an R	87
Molasses	88
With Love, Casserole (AKA, Twenty-Three-Year-Old Becomes Stepmum To A Teenager)	89
Swallowed Whole	93
18 October 1999	95

SECTION II

First Return	101
My Place in The Spiral	103
Measured In Coffee Cups	106
Re-Journey	110
Marking Miles in Kilometers	112
Cycle of Return	114
Fish and Chips	117
Take Me to the Cape	118
Resplendent Breath	123
Awake	126
Formation, December 2016	128
Slipping into Home	133
Uncanny	136

SECTION III

We Arrive at the Water's Edge	147
Tracing Lines	149
Hello, My Name Is Rebecca, and I'm a Settler	151
Voice From the Past	161
Oceans in Us	163
Remainder Reminders	170
Unfurling Frond	172
A - *Gasp* - Feminist	175
The Letter Bee	185

Spiral	189
Pennsylvania Past	191
Touching History	195
Memorandum	198
Time Travel	201
Time to Face It	203
Short-e /e/ Becomes /I/	209
Do You Have Your Camera?	212
Epilogue	225

Works in this collection previously appeared in the literary journals *Two Cities Review* "Echo of Myself," *Poetry NZ* "Molasses," and *Gold Man Review* "Formation."

Portions of the essay "My Place in the Spiral" appear in my memoir *My Place in the Spiral,* Atmosphere Press, 2021.

AUTHOR'S NOTE

This is a hybrid work of creative nonfiction. In these pages you will find essays, vignettes, poems, photographs, and experimental forms all employed to tell my story, to pull moments in, through, and beyond time out from my memories. All events depicted in this book are true to the best of my memory. Most dialog is shown in italics to indicate it is a near-to-true remembered version of what was said.

Our lives, our stories, are not linear. *Te torino haere whakamua, whakamuri* in Māori means: At the same time as the spiral is going forward, it is returning. The spiral is also a way to view time. I was raised in an American culture and society that looked forward – always forward – not back. When I read that Oceania cultures valued the past to understand the present it was there that I found the theory, terminology, and foundation for an understanding of time that made sense to me. It wasn't Western linear time, but circular time and later the spiral time that would bring me into a new understanding of myself and the world around me.

The spiral creates the space for time – past, present, future – to meld together. This book, like the spiral of time, brings together moments when it is the right time and not necessarily in chronological order. Embrace the spiral, dear reader, and journey through time with me.

PROLOGUE:
BLANK SLATE/WHITE BAG

In my twelfth-grade art class, we were assigned the white bag project. Mr. Kraft was always coming up with odd projects for us – one year, we walked into the fine arts studio to find mannequins hanging from the ceiling (study of form); another year, he decided to ink a dead bird he found outside the studio. (My paper still had some entrails lingering near the right wing). But this year – the white bag. Our assignment was to illustrate a bag that would represent a product that said something about ourselves.

I sat at my art table, looking at the blank bag, feeling blank. I looked up at David, a friend since elementary school and a fellow art major, and he was already sketching his design – a fox. Of course, his last name was Fox. A name.

My name? A product?

I left that day with a white bag and sketchbook. That night, while flipping through *Seventeen*, I noticed an ad for Ralph Lauren's Lauren. The simple square burgundy bottle with a gold cap and "Lauren" in gold script. A perfume bottle with my name – yes. I could already see the design – a blue, round-shaped bottle with a wave-like cap in dark blue. Water, ocean waves – the elements that sing to my soul. I sketched it out, but there was a problem: Becky.

My name didn't hold the same elegance of the bottle. Becky made it look like the ever-cheerful Bonnie Bell – most certainly not the caliber of Lauren. It also didn't have the same movement as a wave. No flow. No elegance. No mystery like the sea. I looked around my room for inspiration. Maybe a different word would work, but it needed to represent me. Maybe just Ocean. No, too on the nose. I then observed a rubber stamp sitting on my desk that my sister gave me for my birthday. The stamp was simple: my given name.

Rebecca.

The white-bag project started the movement towards reclaiming my name.

ABOUT THE PRODUCT

Rebecca by Rebecca is a fresh and refined classic fragrance that captures the essence and style of a world-traveling woman: independent, introspective, impassioned. This is a unique mixture of sea, forest, and floral. The bouquet greets the senses with evergreen and citrus top notes of bergamot and juniper berries.

The heart contains whispers of a long-forgotten cottage garden in the trio of rosehip, lavender, and the unusual addition of raspberry.

A luxurious base of salt sea air and oakmoss roots the fragrance to the place where the forest meets the ocean.

Occasion: Day, Night.

Type: *Eau De Toilette.*

"But I don't want to go among mad people," Alice remarked.

"Oh, you can't help that," said the Cat: "we're all mad here. I'm mad. You're mad."

"How do you know I'm mad?" said Alice.

"You must be," said the Cat, "or you wouldn't have come here."

**- LEWIS CARROLL,
ALICE'S ADVENTURES IN WONDERLAND (1865)**

A Pākehā, an American wearing a kahu huruhuru,
a kākahu adorned with feathers.

How did I get here?

SECTION I

"Who in the world am I? Ah, that's the great puzzle!"

**— LEWIS CARROLL,
ALICE'S ADVENTURES IN WONDERLAND (1865)**

MAY 25, 1991

My brother Dwayne sits at the dining room table. Mountains of containers of fruit, vegetables, cheeses, and ring bologna creates a divide between us. It is unseasonably hot for the end of May. I am a month away from graduating High School. We both shine with sweat from carrying all the boxes of food into the house.

Back at the church's Youth Center, we change out of our wedding clothing into our lightweight clothes before cleaning up after our sister's wedding. Mom catered the whole thing, which means Dwayne and I are part of the setting up and tearing down crew. At home, we are the brawn to carry all the boxes. Dad latches the lock on the screen door so it doesn't slam into us each time we walk in, providing the means for opportunist flies to venture in and buzz lazily around the kitchen.

All the cars are unloaded; we sit down for a moment waiting for the next round of instructions from Mom. I stand up, my shin resting on the chair so I can see Dwayne while I complain about the hideous pink floral dress my sister made me wear. Commiserating over all the work we just had to do for the wedding. Clearly, we both thought there were better things to be doing.

Dragging a gallon of iced tea off the table, lifting it to his lips, he takes long gulps. Not looking at me but at the iced tea lid flicking around his fingers, he says, *I better have an important role in your wedding.*

He is a bit miffed that his only role in our sister Amanda's wedding was to announce the bridal party as they enter the reception. He crunches down on a stack of chips, wiping bits of salt off his fingers on the bottom of his white Hawaiian shirt.

Of course, I reply. I pick up the camera sitting on the table. *You'll be the best man.*

Doesn't the guy pick the best man?

I don't care. You will be the best man.

And if he doesn't like it?

Then he shouldn't marry me.

Click. The shutter announces itself. My best man.

I was nineteen when my brother Dwayne died in a farming accident. He fell into the feed mixer after the evening milking, causing multiple injuries to his neck, chest, and legs.

VISION TO VENTURE

Vision to Venture are the words engraved on his headstone. They rest there in granite on the bottom right under:

> Dwayne E. Helm
> May 18, 1966
> Mar. 13, 1992

Yet of the three of Bob and Marilyn Helm's children, I will be the only one to traverse the world. To venture. I will slowly start to untwine myself from the roots sunk deep down in the clay soil of Bucks County, Pennsylvania. I take my twisting stem that marks me as Pennsylvania German and weave myself in and out of the known and the unknown until I am able to unknot myself from my root system and leave the land that holds my ancestors in cemeteries from German Lutheran Cemetery in Philadelphia to St. John's Lutheran on Sleepy Hollow Rd in Spinnerstown. I will wander and find places to hold me and become home. Aotearoa New Zealand. Bellingham, Washington. But none of this would have happened without my brother.

March 13, 1992, unrooted me. Loosened the soil that

bonded me to Pennsylvania but still holds Dwayne. It wasn't a vision that caused me to venture; it was a life lost in an instant that spurred me to move on and into myself.

I THEE WED...AND WITH IT I BESTOW ALL OF THE TREASURES

November 1996

Geoff and I marry at 2 p.m. in a park with sunbathers, tourists, and businesspeople regretting that they must return to the office after enjoying lunch in the warmth of early summer. I am twenty-three and still wide-eyed. Geoff seems so world-wise and at ease with himself – I will understand his place in the world when I reach thirty-eight, the age he is on this day. I am still new to New Zealand and continue to rely on Geoff, as a local, to help me navigate Auckland. It's Thursday – Thanksgiving Day in the United States, my favorite holiday because it means a day with my Aunt Pat and her family. Plus, in November, New Zealand is on the cusp of summer. Geoff likes the idea of getting married on a holiday to make the remembering easier. I didn't learn this until later or I would have informed him, the Kiwi, that the actual date of Thanksgiving changes from year to year.

This Thursday in Auckland, I am without my family – they are in Pennsylvania preparing to celebrate a day of thanks. I am singular in this union. No mother to cry over me, no father to take my hand, no sibling to toast to my marriage.

But the trees are here. Amongst the expansive branches is the space within the city where I feel connection – safe. A few new friends and Geoff's son join us under the Moreton Bay fig. Our tree. Our Thursday. Our city.

ROCKING AND ROLLING

Baby me rocks myself to sleep. Wood wheels roll grooves into yellow pine floorboards. Guests ask, *What's that racket?* Mom forces a smile and pronounces, *That's just Becky rocking.* When language lands on my tongue, I inform my parents when it is time for bed.

Diploma in my hand, I announce I am not going to college – just yet. Travel first. Six months in Scotland. Overtoun House, my little Dumbarton castle. Sharp green crags for my wanderings. I try my best to avoid the sheep shit. When I decide I want to join the theater, I inform my parents I am moving to Ontario, Canada.

I move to Canada on a day when Niagara Falls freezes into claw-like sheets of ice reaching over the edge. Yet, I can still hear the water raging underneath. A range of classes marks my calendar with an eye towards plays. However, the subtle movements – a flick of the wrist, a curl of the finger – seduce me to dance. Ballet – all forms and rules – speaks to my incessant need for order. My instructor says, *You could have been a dancer, but you're too old.* I call my parents and tell them I am moving to Montana.

My life revolves around the seasons of Flathead Lake. I teach preschoolers when I'm not dancing. Midnight dock walks to carve our names into weathered wood. Summer days on the calm, glassy lake balancing our bodies as we descend into canoes. I decide winters of frozen nose hairs and summers of grizzly bears are no longer for me. I tell my parents I'm going to school – Slippery Rock on the other side of Pennsylvania.

Thanksgiving break, snowy drive home on Interstate 80. I rehearse with my dormmate what I will say. Kathleen and I arrive in Quakertown to coffee and cherry pie. *Does Mom already know?* We say good-night. I reverse back to the family room and address my parents as they sit in blue and pink winged chairs. *I met a guy from New Zealand.*

Before I bound up the stairs, I turn at the door and proclaim, *He is coming to visit. And when he is here, I'd like to get my ring, Grammy's diamond, out of the safe deposit box.* Silence, but Mom nods in response. I run up the wooden stairs, skipping over the fourth from the top because it creaks. I walk into my childhood room and open my suitcase over the grooves I once dug into the floorboards with my crib wheels.

UPRIGHT

YOUR ANCESTORS ARE WITH YOU, GUIDING YOU. STOP AND LISTEN TO THEIR WISDOM FOR IT WILL SET YOU ON THE RIGHT PATH.

REVERSED

WATCH OUT! YOU ARE OUT OF ALIGNMENT WITH YOUR TRUE SELF. YOU HAVE MOVED TOO FAR FROM YOUR CENTER.

BECKY

My parents grew up in households where the children all had nicknames or shortened versions of their names. My dad, Robert, became Bob. And to his siblings, he was and still is the much-hated name, according to him, Bobby. My mom, Marilyn, was affectionately called Number Two by her father because she was, quite simply, the second child. I never heard my grandfather call her anything else. So, it would follow that my parents' children would have a family nickname or shortened version of their given name. But, no, my parents broke with tradition, or maybe they railed against a house filled with non-given names. My brother, their firstborn, Dwayne, always remained Dwayne – never Wayne or Dewey, no matter how much Pop-pop tried to turn Dwayne into Dewey. Much later in life, when he was full-grown and living outside our house, the name Janey Edward was sometimes used when talking about Dwayne, mimicking a little girl who struggled to pronounce my brother's name. She called him Jane. No matter how many times we tried to correct her, she'd respond, No, look at my face. It is Jane. My sister, the middle child, our version of number two, Amanda, never dabbled with Mandy or Manda. She was never called Number Two. When she was in high school, our immediate family sometimes called her Panda Bear, but this was not a name she wrote on school reports, and it never left our house.

Then along came me. The child that wasn't supposed to be. A miracle baby? No, I wouldn't go that far. Instead, I was unexpected because the doctors informed my mother that she most likely wouldn't have any more children after my sister was born. And I wonder if the thought crossed my parents' minds that they had a boy and a girl – did they need another child? Should they be happy and blessed with the two they had? My mom had two siblings, and my dad had three siblings. So, maybe they had visions of keeping with their respective size of families. And that whisper of hope for one more baby turned into my arrival.

Born on a snowy day in February, my parents considered calling me Heather, but Dad added one more vote for my name because it was easier to spell. I was named Rebecca Jean Helm. Jean for my mother's aunt, but we later found out she spelled it Jeanne. I swiftly became Becky. And sometimes Dad called me Becca Jean. But Becky was the name on all my school papers. The name I learned to write, occasionally with a backward K, when I started to learn the alphabet and that those individual letters formed words. I often liked to spell

My first memoir – age six

out our names. Even now, I hear Mom's voice slowly spelling out my siblings' names as I wrote them, tongue out in concentration, in crayon in my coloring book resting on the wooden pew at church. D.W.A.Y.N.E and A.M.A.N.D.A. There was a singsong way she said each letter, and that is how I say them in my head each time I write their names. And me? B.E.C.K.Y.

My golden blonde, almost strawberry curls pulled back into two pigtails and shiny blue eyes fit the cutesy name Becky. I was sunshine in dresses and knee socks. Then my hair turned brown, my unruly curls cut off. I became Becky, tom-boy, in overalls or pants, scabbed chin or knees depending on how the tumble went down. Bossy and often single-minded, I stomped through the world around me. I went from being Miss Prissy to Bossy Pants; however, I'd argue they are the same thing, just viewed with a different lens. But even with my tendency toward knowing my own mind, I was (and remain) a rule follower. I wanted to be the star pupil, the golden child, the best friend. I grew up in the Mennonite church, and more than anything, I wanted to be a model of the church that molded me.

The Mennonite Church was prominent in my life. It was my heritage, a family narrative deeply rooted in our role of bringing the Mennonite faith to Pennsylvania. The first group of Mennonites, with Quakers, to arrive in America came from Germany in 1683. In *An Introduction to Mennonite History*, Cornelius J. Dyck provides details on the early Mennonite Church in America:

> *About 1690 elections were held in which William Rittenhouse was chosen as the first minister [. . .] Following the death of Rittenhouse the Germantown assistant minister Jacob Gottschalk baptized eleven members and served the Lord's Supper. That same year the small congregation built a log meetinghouse in Germantown, which was replaced in 1770 by a stone building which is still in use.*

Rev. Jacob Gottschalk (other name variations include Jakob Gaedschalk and Jacob van der Heggen) was the first Bishop of the American Mennonite Church, and my eighth great-grandfather. Gottschalk was not part of the first group of Mennonites to arrive in Pennsylvania on invitation from William Penn; instead, he came to America around 1701. According to Ronald J. Hunsicker, *Growing Up Gottshall*, "On June 11, 1701, he (Gottschalk) received a letter from the Church of Goch granting him and his family permission to migrate to Pennsylvania... [by] October 8, 1702, Jacob Gaedschalk was ordained as a minister along with Hans Neuss to serve with William Rittenhouse." A spreading collection of family lines connected my life to Gottschalk's. It is common to see our family name in stained glass windows and on plaques throughout Pennsylvania's Mennonite churches.

I spent a lot of time in the Church, where I was trained about my role as a girl. In eighth grade, I was baptized and became a member of the church. The Mennonites, an Anabaptist sect formed during the Protestant Reformation, believed that children shouldn't be baptized because they could not decide about their faith in God. Instead, we dedicated infants. The parents promised to raise the child in the ways of the Lord, the church pledged to be the example of Christ for the child, and then we would eat some cake.

Every Wednesday night, I went to Pioneer Girls, where we were taught crafts, sewing, cooking. They were making us into homemakers living in community with other women of the faith. As with most religions, the Mennonite way of life comes with rules – a haven for rule followers. I melded and molded myself into who people wanted me to be. My life goals echoed my upbringing; my ambitions went as far as becoming a wife and mother, preferably in the near future. And maybe someday a teacher, but before I would go to college, I needed to be a missionary, the ultimate sign of my faith. For our high school yearbook, we were asked to share our next steps. Most people wrote about college, degrees, jobs, but for my response to Class of 1991: Future plans, I wrote, "will do missionary work and attend college."

***

Early in the 1990s, I graduated from high school and started, as I stated in my yearbook, my life as a missionary. I lived in Dumbarton, Scotland; Cambridge, Ontario; and Lakeside, Montana, with a mission organization called Youth with a Mission. Often months passed until a move to a new location and mission. During these months, I worked at the Provident Bookstore, a local Mennonite bookstore in Souderton, Pennsylvania. I worked in the book department, which meant days of pulling and shelving books. Somehow my months home always seemed to fall around returns, where we would take inventory and pull any books that were not selling to return to the vendor. Sometimes we worked in pairs and sometimes we were given a sheet of paper and a section of shelves to work on by ourselves.

There was a tiny section, only two shelves of a bookshelf section, of psychology books. One night, while pulling returns in the psychology section, I noticed a book on names and the attributes people associate with names. Curious, I looked up Becky. According to the book and the people surveyed for it, Becky was bubbly, friendly, kind. She wore overalls. That seemed very specific, but there it was in black and white, a bit of a tomboy, climbing trees. Basically, Becky was a sweet, down-to-earth person who liked to laugh and cared about animals. Okay, I thought. I guessed it was somewhat accurate. I flipped the pages to find Rebecca. The book described someone named Rebecca as sophisticated, stylish, intelligent. Rebecca wore glasses and had a sense of authority about her. At that moment, I realized I didn't want to be a Becky. I wanted to be a Rebecca. I wanted a life like I just read about in the R section of the name book. If this was true, why would I want to be bubbly Becky in overalls when I could be sophisticated, stylish Rebecca?

I started to tell people I wanted to go by Rebecca. That request was basically ignored. I was Becky, and Becky I would remain. As a missionary moving to different places regularly, I had the luxury of starting over; I was away from home and from those who knew me as Becky. On the journey, I'd remind myself that I am Rebecca now; however, I'd always cave under the pressure of my name. I'd introduce myself as Rebecca, and if they asked – and they always asked – *Do you go by Becky?* Could they see it in my face the bubbly, overall-wearing Becky? No matter how I tried to present myself. I'd answer *Yes*. Or *You can call me Becky.*

***

Back at the Provident Bookstore, working at the registers this time instead of the book department, I was biding my time waiting for another move. This move, however, was not part of a mission trip. Instead, I was moving to New Zealand to marry a Kiwi I met online on mIRC, internet relay chat in 1995. One of the high school students working with me on a busy Saturday said, *Hey, you're going to be BB. Becky Beardsall.* I snapped back, *No! I will be Rebecca Beardsall.* Determined this would be the moment, it was finally my time to move into the person I wanted to be, not the one I was told to be. I needed to let Becky go. I left her in Pennsylvania when I boarded my flight in Newark, heading to LA enroute to Auckland.

My complete transition to actualizing the Rebecca persona I read about in the book would take years. Still, my rebirth happened when I walked out of that international terminal and Geoffrey welcomed me home. Auckland, New Zealand, became my place for renewal. I had just as many growth stages to work through before I could fully claim Rebecca as myself.

BEYOND BECKY

I often feel as if my life is a spiral, moving in and out of various moments in time and back again. Time is my map to navigate my life.

I met my dear friend Athena when she was interviewing for a job on my team at Western Washington University. She arrived with Storiarts red Macbeth writing/reading gloves and a bag full of handmade journals. I immediately wanted to stop the interview and ask her to be my friend. She didn't get the job. However, a few months later, she accepted another position in the same department that I worked for on campus. Of course, we became fast friends with a passion for reading and all things paper. One day, Athena introduced me to *Wisdom of the Oracle* cards by Colette Baron-Reid. People would walk into Athena's office throughout the day and ask to pull a card, hoping to find some meaning to the day's events or the actions needed to dislodge from the feeling of being stagnant. I, diving into all things Athena, purchased my own box of divination cards. I marched through 2019, asking the cards to guide me. On the last day of 2019, my husband and I pulled twelve cards to take us through 2020.

Our 2020 started with grief as we had to say goodbye to our beautiful, old-soul, British shorthair cat Myrtle a mere eight hours after pulling our years' worth of divination cards. Twelve months later, the great conjunction of Juniper and Saturn, the closest they had been seen together in four centuries, coincided with the winter solstice. As someone who didn't always pay attention to the planets and stars, I first ignored all the alerts popping up on my social media about The Great Conjunction. However, when Colette Baron-Reid, author of the *Wisdom of the Oracle* cards, posted about a free online Winter Solstice celebration with astrologer Jennifer Racioppi, my interest was piqued. I signed up for the workshop on December 21, 2020, hoping to learn more about this great conjunction which had everyone abuzz. Racioppi started talking about charts and planets, and I immediately felt lost. When she mentioned that something depended on where Aquarius was on your own chart, I realized I couldn't even begin comprehending what they were talking about. I knew I was an Aquarius. The basic magazine version of sun signs was what I really knew of astrology. I knew how to look for my birth date lumped into a range of dates that accompany most magazine, newspaper, and online horoscopes.

The summer of 2019, I learned about sun signs, moon signs, and rising signs when a student working for my unit thought I was a Scorpio. At the time, I thought I was a Scorpio ascending (rising), but I had the time of my birth wrong. Soon afterward, learning about sun, moon, and rising signs, Athena and I started talking about getting our natal charts read, but we never followed through. However, after the workshop with Racioppi, I decided it was something I needed to do, even if it meant doing it on my own without Athena.

I knew I wanted to get my chart read, but I didn't know how to do this until a fellow writer, Twila, who I met at the Association of Writers and Writing Programs (AWP) conference in

Portland, posted on Facebook that her sister did natal charts.

January 2021, I had my natal chart read. I sat in a session as a yogi-philosopher eerily told me about my life. This moment created a shift in my life that I wasn't quite prepared for as I rather innocently walked into the web of my natal wheel without any real knowledge or the understanding of astrology.

I reached out and soon I found myself on Skype listening to where the planets were situated at the exact moment of my birth. The map of me. I learned about terms like grand trine, yod, Midheaven (the MC), north node, south node. I watched and rewatched our recorded session, searching for more information and clarity.

In typical fashion, I went to books. I read about the houses of astrology, the roles of planets, and the wound of Chiron. I listened to podcasts on astrology, and it was while listening to Jessica Lanyadoo's *Ghost of a Podcast* that I learned about Midheaven and the tenth house. In episode 196, Lanyadoo states, "the Midheaven is what you show to the world." Midheaven is also called the middle sky and is situated on the tenth house cusp. The tenth house is all about career and public standing – profession, ambition, aspiration. It is also about how others perceive you and your status in the community. I listened to Lanyadoo talk about Midheaven while I washed dishes after dinner. My hands full of suds dropped the pan back in the hot water, and I pushed the headphones closer to my ears to make sure I heard her correctly,

> So the Midheaven is your tenth house cusp, but the tenth house itself, it points to your life's mission; it points to your sense of direction. The tenth house is the place **where we get information about the kind of pressures that were placed upon us in our early developmental years, so our parents, our grandparents, our guardians kind of were like this is**

> **how you should be in the world; this is how adults should be in the world; this is the kind of expectations we have of how you're going to show up in the world and what you're allowed to do.** (emphasis mine)

This was the narrative of Becky, who she was told to be. A good Mennonite girl, which meant knowing my place in society and, more specifically, my position in the clearly established patriarchal society. As most Mennonite girls will explain, we are raised and trained to be wives and mothers. We started looking for future husbands when we were in high school. If a girl isn't married by twenty-two, she's considered an old maid. Therefore, around twenty, the panic of not finding a husband sets in: as such, when I was nineteen and living in Scotland, all I could talk about was finding a husband to the complete confusion of all the other women around me. They would tell me – *You're so young. You have plenty of time to worry about getting married.* But I didn't know how else to fit into the world. There was no other direction or guidance. Becky was trying to find her place in the world while honoring the expectations of her parents and grandparents. She was following the call of Christ as a missionary – the least God could do was provide her with a husband. Maybe even a missionary husband to slake her thirst for travel, adventure, and change. To fill the deep hole of not belonging to the place where she was born.

On March 19, 2021, I woke up with the strangest sensation. It was a mixture of recognition and dissociation at the same time. What caused this awkward space was a name, quite simply – Becky Helm. It was familiar and foreign. I had forgotten that it was the name I used to go by. I hadn't heard that name in over twenty years, but for some reason, it was the first word that popped into my head when I woke up that morning. I looked up at the light streaming in from the window above my bed, filtered by the sheer curtain. A softness needed to ease into the day. Squinting my eyes, not at the sun, but the name lingering: Becky Helm. Why did she come to me now? Who was she? I purposely erased her, but here she sat, waiting for me.

I tried to ignore her sitting there on the edge of the bed, but she whispered that I needed to acknowledge her. I promptly got out of bed; on a day I was meant to sleep in; it was Geoff's birthday, and we took the day off together to celebrate. Waiting for my laptop to wake up, I thought about my next steps. Propelled forward with Becky sitting in the background, I typed up a message and sent it out via email and Facebook. I reached out to people from my earlier life and asked them who they thought Becky Helm was; I stated this could be a list of attributes, adjectives, or a sentence or two. But I wanted to know who she was and how had she presented herself to the world. A range of answers came flooding back, with the memories:

- Giggly and fun.
- The Becky Helm I knew was always one of the kindest people you'd ever want to meet. Kinda quiet, but once you got to know her, actually very talkative. She was always smiling, often giggling, and generally making the mood a positive and welcoming one. You looked forward to seeing her because you'd be in a better mood after you saw her. I remember her being pretty devoted to her faith, too, if I am remembering correctly. She was really great.
- Becky Helm was a strong and independent person. When other kids picked on me, she was always there to help me stand up for myself.

- I found Becky Helm to be a very nice, quiet girl.
- Crazy, lovely, bubbly, lively, amazing laugh.
- Curious, intuitive, independent, fun, loyal, adventuresome.
- Becky Helm was quite shy and reserved, but a people watcher. A deep and creative person.
- Becky Helm was my absolutely fun friend. I knew you were good people because you went to church, but you were kind and funny and creative.
- Sweet, kind, caring, good sense of humor, cheerful, related well to children – understanding what they liked to do given their age level, dependable, and trustworthy.
- I remember Becky Helm as funny, entertaining, and creative, and a fierce friend – you even tried to get me to stay above the fray a few years later.
- Becky Helm seemed happy, perky, and positive.
- I always found Becky Helm to be wise and very level-headed. She had a way of sharing truth kindly. I always remember watching Becky with her close friends. Becky, Bonnie, Tracy, and Denise always had the best time, and I always remember wanting to be a part of it.

Here I was, written in words of school friends, church leaders, and summer camp acquaintances. Becky was happy, giggly, perky, and friendly. She was also quiet and reserved. A few people mentioned Becky as being religious and part of the church. This was Becky. The Becky my family, my church, my community, wanted me to be. It is not that she isn't still part of me, but there is a layer here of a person who wasn't quite me. I was, and am, more complex than the down-to-earth, friendly, bubbly Becky. But I played my role well for a while.

In my journey through navigating my natal chart, I learned that Chiron, the wounded healer sometimes referred to as the core wound, points to some kind of pain, trauma that we are charged to work through while on earth. In my natal chart session, Chiron was linked to my childhood home. I didn't quite understand how that could be because I had a good, safe childhood as a member of a kind and loving family. The yogi-philosopher reading my chart tried again to explain the position of Chiron on my chart. *Well, I never felt like I really belonged. Kind of like a West Coast person raised on the East Coast,* I replied to her probing. She confirmed that could exactly be it. After my session, I thought about not belonging a bit more.

My childhood, while good, always felt a little off. I tried hard to be the person the community wanted me to be, but I knew this wasn't right deep down. A simple example of this was around the time my sister was getting married. My sister and mom were in my room. I told them I wanted a husband who would fight with me. They looked at me in shock. I tried to explain in my limited vocabulary and understanding of the wide world outside of the Mennonite lens. I wanted someone to challenge me intellectually, and I most certainly didn't want to be the submissive wife. I could see them struggling to understand me and felt like I was speaking in another language, so I just stopped talking.

Is it any wonder people thought I was shy and quiet?

This was often my response to the world around me – silence. I found it safer in my mind instead of sharing my honest thoughts and desires with the people around me. In her book *Cosmic Health*, Jennifer Racioppi states that the message for someone with their Chiron in Aries is: "you are here to learn sovereignty and how to self-authorize without needing approval from others." My shift away from and final break from Becky started me on the road of self-authorization, even if I didn't realize it at that moment.

It wasn't until I received an email from one of my close friends that I finally felt seen, understood, and validated in my belief that Becky was a whole other person to who I am today.

My friend wrote me this email in response to my prompt – Who was Becky Helm:

> Huh. Becky Helm. I haven't heard that name in a long time.
>
> When I think of Becky Helm, I first think Mennonite. I think that because I knew Becky Helm through my connections at Mennonite Church and Mennonite Camp and her family are long-standing Mennonite people. And Mennonites are good people. God-fearing people who serve others. Becky Helm followed suit in my eyes. She came from a stable family and followed the rules and was a healthy, stable person, and I liked that steadiness in her.
>
> Becky Helm was a good friend to me when I was a teen. She was the person I looked forward to seeing at church. I looked for her and we went to Sunday School together and we both were interested in learning more about God and the Bible. We sat together up front and loved Florence Dietz [our high school Sunday School teacher] and didn't have a lot of tolerance for the screwballs who were in the youth group fraternizing with each other. Becky Helm was deeper than them. She was reflective and introspective and thoughtful, and I felt like I could actually talk to her about deeper things. I remember her being a good listener and conversationalist, not afraid to go deep and ponder.

Becky Helm was creative. She always had a little artsy edge to her decorating style and dress, and that was fun. She liked flowers. I remember being at Camp Men-o-lan as counselors in side-by-side cabins and took our breaks together and talked about boys and Becky picked the flowers around the camp. She was kind of whimsical like that. And she kept a journal then. I remember us taking breaks and writing in journals.

I also remember Becky being fun. We had a LOT of great laughs together with our group of 5 friends. When I think about the personalities of each member of our little group, Becky felt like the stable one. It's not like the rest of us were unstable or anything. Becky was just Becky and Bonnie was just Bonnie and Jen was just Jen and Denise was just Denise. And we just all clicked, and it just worked and it was a gift to my youth. Truly. I feel very blessed to have had that group. It really is one of the fondest things about my teen years. And Becky was just part of it. She was there and you just kind of knew what you were going to get with Becky. She was balanced and reasonable. But fun, too. We just had so much fun together, all of us. Becky liked to laugh. We all did.

Becky surprised me when she grew into adulthood, which probably meant that I really didn't know her very well after all, or I wasn't paying attention. She went to YWAM and started dancing and then to college as a creative writing major. I didn't realize that those things were in her. Then she floored us all by marrying a much older man who she met on . . . GASP . . . the internet. I'll never forget the day somebody got a letter at camp one summer we were working there . . . I think it was Jen who got the letter and read it to me. We were all flipping out. She was leaving college and moving to New Zealand to marry an older divorced guy with a kid. We panicked. Who is this Becky Helm?!

So, maybe this Becky Helm as I perceived her growing up has much more in her than I knew, or took the time to know. Suddenly in her early 20s she's a creative artist and writer, a world-traveler, a daring young woman who falls in love and moves across the world. Not safe. Bold. Courageous.

After she returned to the US later, post-25 and thus post the time frame you want me to comment on, I met her again as Rebecca Beardsall. And I fell in love with her for who she was becoming then. It took a while to adjust to not calling her Becky, but honestly, now it feels awkward to call her anything but Rebecca. What a strong, confident, thoughtful, self-assured, intelligent, compassionate, successful, beautiful woman Rebecca has become. Of course, she was all those things as Becky, but Becky was undeveloped Rebecca, wasn't she? How brave of Becky to step into Rebecca.

UNDERSEA CABLES

May 1995

My colleague at Youth with a Mission, Sammy, promised to show me this new technology called the Internet. To do so, we had to go to the one and only office on the decommissioned army base that had a computer. In Lakeside, Montana surrounded by the rugged and spacious beauty of grizzly country, we gathered our chairs around a small, white particle board desk. We gazed at a blank screen and listened to the banshee call of early dial-up. Sammy said the Internet was going to change the world. The half-loaded screen said otherwise. I didn't believe him, or maybe I did – I found it hard to envisage something that couldn't even load in fifteen minutes would change too much. We aborted the mission after twenty minutes. As I walked out of the office into the surprisingly warm spring sun, pine-scented air, bright blue Montana sky, I never imagined the Internet would alter my course – my plan of going to university, earning my degree, and being a star journalist in some big city like Chicago or Seattle.

I arrived at university with a typewriter in August 1995 and left in May 1996 with a computer. Why? Well, because my dorm only had three computers in the lab, and I needed to communicate with someone – a guy, shyly confessed when pressed – I met online. He lived in New Zealand. He owned the first internet lounge in the country.

ECHO OF MYSELF

I keep falling into myself, reverberations
    of me melding into one solid form.
            My limbs lie languid, waving
in the waves that wash
      me toward the shores of a land in the South
    Pacific – not the land of my birth, but the place I call home.
Navigating waters from the Jersey Shore
to Auckland, Orewa, Wai iti to discovery –
that part of myself that belongs
      to the sea goddess – a land
   locked girl from Quakertown knowing all along
that it was the water's
 deep silence calling her –
pulling like the tide tugs the land.
      I never realized every time
    I wrapped my fist around the garden hose nozzle
        soaking the dirt for planting
or felt the grey-green rocks resting
        in the Unami creek under my toes
or begged for another bath, enameled cast

iron haven almost overflowing
      or reaped the punishment for wasting water washing my feet
              in the mossy ground by the side
          of the house – that I was just trying to reach
        back to the beginning
  where I was heading

UPRIGHT

YOUR CURIOSITY IS TAKING YOU TO NEW LEVELS. TREASURES AWAIT. BE PREPARED FOR LOVELY SURPRISES.

CURIOSITY

REVERSED

CURIOSITY CAN TAKE YOU TO PLACES YOU DON'T WANT TO GO. BE ALERT AND KNOW THAT THINGS WILL BE CLEAR SOON.

mIRC – INTERNET RELAY CHAT

/list

/join #friends

\<dread\> hi

\<Andersson\> Welcome, Polgara.

\<hAck\> Hey.

\<lolly\> Hi, Polgara.

\<Polgara\> Hi everyone!

\<Polgara\> Where are you all from?

\<Andersson\> Sweden

\<hAck\> Texas, baby!

\<dread\> nz

\<Polgara\> New Zealand?

\<dread\> yes

/msg \<dread\> Hi. I have friends in CHCH. Where are you in New Zealand?

dread auckland

/msg \<dread\> Cool. I remember looking Auckland up in an encyclopedia with my friend Bonny because her last name is Auckland

/msg \<dread\> What do you do in Auckland?

/msg \<dread\> I'm from Pennsylvania

/msg \<dread\> I am going to school at Slippery Rock University

/msg \<dread\> Am I bothering you?

dread sorry, brb

/msg \<dread\> brb?

dread be right back :)

/msg \<dread\> oh, okay

dread sorry, I was helping a customer.

dread I own an internet café Des has joined #friends

\<Andersson\> Welcome back, Des!

\<dread\> hi

\<hAck\> Des, darlin

\<Polgara\> Hi, Des.

/msg \<dread\> do you always come on this chat channel?

/msg \<dread\> what's with the name dread?

dread I thought it sounded cool.

dread has quit #friends

dread has joined #friends dread has quit #friends

\<Polgara\> Where are you from des?

\<Des\> Cape Town

\<Des\> South Africa dread has joined #friends

\<Andersson\> Welcome back, dread! Having issues with your internet?

\<dread\> busy

dread polgara

/msg \<dread\> yes?

dread I have to go maybe we can talk later

/msg \<dread\> okay.

\<Andersson\> BRB

/msg \<dread\> It was lovely to meet you

/msg \<dread\> Good night! Or is it morning there?

dread 4 in the avro :)

dread saturday

/msg \<dread\> avro?

dread afternoon

/msg \<dread\> 10 pm Friday here

dread nice to meet you

/msg \<dread\> ditto

\<dread\> bye

\<Polgara\> Nice meeting everyone. I'm heading off now.

dread has quit #friends

Polgara has quit #friends

TIME ZONES

By November 1995, I, Polgara, was in a relationship with Geoff (aka Dread, aka Pendragon).

We had shifted from just friends to a cyberspace couple in a month. We only had words, and hours to express them. Without other distractions that normally are part of courtship, we learned a lot about each other and felt that our life journeys were easily melding together. We had an ever-expanding list of topics to explore from religion to world politics, from contemplations of dreams to the quandary over the hopelessness of the word hope. I was challenged on my beliefs and ways I thought about the world. I opened up doorways once shut to me.

<polgara> I feel so free with you

<pendragon> well yes you know it is nice to be able to say what you think

<pendragon> without having to worry about what sort of reception you will receive

<pendragon> I love that about you

<polgara> I love that about you too

<pendragon> we must never lose this

<polgara> no never . . . we cant

<pendragon> we should write it down as one of our guiding principles

I logged on to the computer whenever I had the chance. I glared at people in the computer lab frantically writing their papers. My dreams hijacked by DOS script and all my conversations translated into glowing green text on a black screen. I stayed up late to talk to Geoff. The mixed time zones slowly crushed my will to study. Early one morning my alarm went off for my 8 a.m. class and I didn't hear it because in my dream I desperately typed out my message, to be heard, to get a response from New Zealand.

Thirty minutes later there was a knock on my door, a dorm-mate asking me if I was going to class; pulled out of my computer dream I answered, No. The first time I skipped a class, ever.

An expensive international phone call to hear each other's voice ended up as mainly nervous giggles and comments about each other's accent. I stood with my back pinned to the cold concrete dorm wall and wondered if I would ever meet him in person. We sent photos in the mail and waited. We could say to each other that it didn't matter what each other looked like, because we knew the person inside, but let's be honest here – attraction is always part of the equation. I knew he would look older, because, well, he was – fifteen years– but he didn't look anything like I imagined.

There was one picture of the five or six he sent to me that I said *That's him*. That's the person I want to be with. I still have the photo . . . Geoff on a green park bench, Albert Park maybe, him looking completely relaxed; his ocean blue eyes gazing into the lens and a smile, I know intimately now, developing. A shirt that I'd never see him wear, a swirl of reds and blues.

He still has his favorite of my first photos in a frame on his desk. Me on the stairs of my childhood home, where my parents no longer live. My mom's collection of antique Americana pottery placed on every other step. A black turtleneck and jeans, and bare feet in the middle of winter.

My parents were not surprised when I stood before them in our formal family room of colonial blue and English tea rose furniture and announced I met someone in New Zealand. I wasn't the first in the family to run off to marry a man overseas. My mother's younger sister, Pat, flew to Ansbach,

Germany to get married without telling her father, a widower, her intentions. They all saw that side of my nature from the moment I arrived in the world.

WEDDING DAY

Thursday in the warmth of early summer of Auckland I stand next to Geoff under the Moreton Bay. I am without my family – they are in Pennsylvania.

    I tell my family not to come. My parents and my sister-in-law Tracey want to be here with me. I say that it wouldn't be fair if only they flew to New Zealand and my sister, without the financial means to travel to the other side of the world, remains at home. I claim fairness as the motive, but really it is my brother. If Dwayne can't be here, I don't want anyone. I promised him. I assured him of the best man-ship – an echo of failure to uphold my end of a deal.

It weighs me down, walking through the sun and shadows to the spot under the long limbs of the fig tree. Dwayne's presence lingers behind me in the white scarf fluttering in the sea breeze, tugging against my neck. I feel him here among the limbs and leaves. He is my best man, and the only person from my family I allow into this day of sunshine, sunflowers, and nervous giggles.

HEART OF STEEL

Heart of winter in Pennsylvania, Geoff tells me about the sweltering summer and Christmases at the beach. Work stories of cranes, trucks, blast furnaces, smelters, and slag sound familiar. I grew up in the shadow of Bethlehem Steel. Steel that built America. I try to place him amongst the dark and fiery stacks.

Geoff takes me to Glenbrook Steel Mill, which doesn't look anything like the steel mill nestled in the hills of Lehigh County. Waiuku seems small and quaint. Where are the miles of row homes? Where are the old brick office blocks? Instead, we walk black sand beaches. A two-story pub with wrapping verandas—the Kentish Hotel, New Zealand's oldest licensed pub—is where Rebecca has her first beer.

RING OF FIRE

Ruapehu spewed ash into the air when I arrived in New Zealand in 1996. My decision to move to New Zealand had been an easy one – I withdrew from university in May and started shipping fragments of my life– books, clothing, CDs, pictures – to Auckland in June. My flight booked for July 19.

Geoff came to Pennsylvania to meet me in February. We looked at engagement rings in Philadelphia but decided to go with my grandmother's ring. My paternal grandfather gave it to me when I was sixteen. Pop-pop often stopped by our house to spend some time with our cat and to see us, I guess. The day he arrived with the ring I led him out to the backyard where Magee, my black and white cat, sat in the grass. Pop-pop patted my head, as if I were Magee, his standard sign of affection for his grandchildren, and handed me a box. He wanted me to have Grammy's ring because I was the only granddaughter left without a diamond. A delicate ring with three small diamonds set in platinum with a yellow gold band. I doubt that Pop-pop ever imagined that the ring he gave his love would be placed on my finger on a bridge overlooking the Auckland skyline, sparkling in the evening sky. New Zealand never crossed his Pennsylvania-German mind. We had the band switched to

The Unfurling Frond

platinum before I tucked the velvet-lined box into my carryon bag.

My flight out of Philadelphia was delayed because of lightning. Held in the death grips of Bucks County, land of my birth, meant I missed my flight out of LAX. I had a long, lonely night in Los Angeles to ponder the loss of my home in Pennsylvania and time to worry about what awaited me in New Zealand. Moments before I drifted off to sleep, I heard about Ruapehu coming back to life.

As the pilot circled Auckland, he mentioned that there were around sixty volcanoes in the area. This was news to me, as Geoff had assured me that Ruapehu was far away from Auckland. *A four-hour drive,* he said. But he hadn't mentioned these other volcanoes. I lacked concrete knowledge of volcanoes. The closest I came to learn about volcanoes was the Plaster of Paris one we made in third grade. A chemical reaction produced a messy foam that oozed down the sides of our perfectly produced cone. Or the glass jar of ash from the 1980 Mount St. Helens eruption, an event that coincided with my aunt and uncle's visit to the West Coast, and they brought home some of the ash they brushed off their camper.

The pilot never told us the volcanoes near Auckland were dormant, nor did he teach us about the Ring of Fire. Only later did I learn about the Ring of Fire and the surreal landscape made by pumice. The Ring of Fire consists of a string of 75% of the world's volcanoes (one of the more active volcanoes is Ruapehu) and is the meeting point of multiple tectonic plates that continually slide and collide into or under each other34T. The Ring of Fire spans from South America to New Zealand. It isn't really a ring, but a squiggly U, almost horseshoe shaped.

Tectonic plates shudder to restructure the earth and the edges of the Pacific Ocean as 90% of the world's earthquakes occur around the ring. Unbeknownst to me, I arrived at the edge of the alive and fluctuating horseshoe – a ring.

Mesmerized by the surreal green landscape, I watched as

the hills seemed to roll on top of each other like waves. And water, I had never seen so much water. Coming from landlocked Pennsylvania, I wasn't expecting all the water, layers of blues previously only witnessed in National Geographic magazines. These waters provided the calmness I sought.

PIECES OF ME

Bright green, gnarled trees and the vibrating hum of Auckland – cars, people, machinery – greeted me. I walked into the apartment, our apartment, dropped my suitcase by the door, and took off my shoes to the welcome coolness of the white tiles. The galley-style kitchen, the lounge with pinkish wool carpet, the bathroom – the size of a bedroom – with the laundry tucked behind the door. My books carefully placed along the walls of the lounge, set up like dominos ready to be tipped over, ended at the blue wooden table. My clothing, shipped down prior to my arrival, was perfectly folded, a skill I never mastered but continue to admire of Geoffrey. He had arranged them in the dresser drawers. I found pieces of my life on display throughout the one-bedroom apartment in Auckland. Geoff created a space for me to return to my things, to our home.

We didn't emerge or leave the apartment until hunger drove us into the night.

Geoff took me away from the lights of Queen Street into a dark alleyway between a carpark and an old building. I asked where we were going, and he mentioned something about food. It seemed unlikely that we were going to find food in an alley, but I followed him. We walked under a rusty fire escape and up a set of stairs to a door with a yellow light next to it. It turned out to be a café. DKD, one of Auckland's first cafes, started in 1984. Chrome Formica-topped tables and red and orange vinyl-covered chairs left over from the 50s peppered the dark, dimly lit café. I experienced my first flat white at DKD. The lore of the city claimed DKD was where the flat white was invented.

The flat white's strong, caramel-like coffee and microfoam washed over and lingered on my tongue. I looked at Geoffrey. I understood captivation.

CLIMBING BRANCHES

I recognize trees in Aotearoa New Zealand as if they were old friends. Each trip home I return to the trees that brought me through my transition from Pennsylvania to Aotearoa New Zealand. Specifically, the trees in Albert Park. I talk to them. They place me.

Albert Park – my haven in Auckland. Whenever we walk the city streets, I know a green, lush world, hidden, awaits. I beg to remove ourselves from the traffic and noise to go through Albert Park. A detour between our first apartment and my favorite bookstore, Whitcoulls, on the corner of Victoria and Queen Streets.

As a kid growing up in Quakertown, I didn't look at trees as anything extraordinary except for the fact that they create the oxygen I need to breathe – thank you, grade school science. In the autumn their colors paint the Pennsylvania landscape. And every time I walk out of the house in Montana the sharp smell of conifers hit me. Other than that, a tree is a tree is a tree.

This all changes in Aotearoa New Zealand. My love affair with trees starts on my second day in Auckland when Geoff takes me to Albert Park. I grab Geoff's arm and whisper, as if to speak aloud is sacrilegious. *Look at the trees. They're magic.*

We sit on a bench, looking at the Moreton Bay fig (*Ficus macrophylla*), and I lean over to Geoff and announce: *They get up and walk around when we are sleeping.* Years later when I read Tolkien, I can easily picture Ents. I know them. They live in Albert Park. I wonder if there is a specific tree that Tolkien had in mind when he wrote about a tree walking and talking. The Moreton Bay fig's thick, expansive branches reach out over the park and its intertwining roots spread over the ground.

***

The ombu (*Phytolacca dioica*) became another favorite place in the park. The ombu, like most of the trees in the park, is not native to Aotearoa New Zealand; it is native to Argentina.

A visit to the grand ombu requires a ritual. One that I create during my first year living in Auckland. I start the journey at the base of our Moreton Bay fig near the gazebo. Past the fountain and up the stairs where I pause to greet her – the statue of Queen Victoria – a statue that was unveiled in 1899 during her 60th Jubilee. I offer a final nod in acknowledgement to the Queen before I continue to my sacred place.

The ombu with its massive branches twisting up towards the sun, its roots on full display, welcomes me home. I climb its roots and find my spot, my body nestling amongst its massive legs, my back resting firmly in its expansive arms.

In the roots, I survey the park. A young boy sits on a bench by the fountain feeding birds. Next to him, on the adjacent bench, an elderly couple sits close together. In the lush green grass, university students read and sunbathe, young professionals eat their lunches. I watch from inside the ombu.

California palms wave in the breeze, and Victoria, her arms folded, glares over the land . . . Māori land.

A tree brought here by Governor Grey is part of New Zealand's history. A keeper of the past, the ombu is a witness to civil war and biculturalism. Its non-native roots find their hold in the soil of Aotearoa. I feel home . . . in a massive tree that most busy Aucklanders just walk by without a second glance. It's safer to sit in the roots instead of being exposed on the sunny benches. Hidden. A secreted space for me to look out over the park and see Auckland from a different perspective. At once I am part of and an observer of the city. The soft wood smell of dirt, bark under my fingernails, ants crawling up my legs bind me to the land just as the ombu roots dig deep down under Auckland. Branch shadows launch me out beyond the concrete as if I am the Cheshire cat, invisible to the world.

EVERYTHING HAS TWO NAMES

I.

My clothing smells like late spring in Pennsylvania. Freshly mown grass, lilac, rose, and the warm musk only the sun can add caught in the fibers of fabric. Frozen and woven in the shirt I pull over my head before heading out to Queen Street on the hunt for a birthday gift for my dad. I buy him a shirt with a rainbow trout and a curving script Aotearoa underneath. I am unsure if my dad will understand that Aotearoa is New Zealand. I don't know if I fully understand it even after Geoff explains it to me.

II.

Our wedding takes place in the middle of Auckland, the largest city in Aotearoa New Zealand. The same park where we get engaged. Where, from my first night in Auckland, we walk toward restoration. We talk about our vision of the future. I love the bright reds of the coral tree (*Erythrina speciosa*), flowering gum (*Eucalyptus ficifolia*), pohutukawa (*Metrosideros excelsa*); the silky white cups of the bull bay magnolia

(*Magnolia grandiflora*); the expansive, twisted branches of the ombu (*Phytolacca dioica*), cork oak (*Quercus suber*); and the willow myrtle (*Agnois flexuosa*) lightning bolt limbs hidden under a veil of green.

    The park boasts over eighty, mainly introduced, species of trees planted before the turn of the century. I make it a point on each visit to stop by the statue of Queen Victoria. Her stoic stance and gaze reminds me I am no longer in Pennsylvania.

III.

Albert Park was once known as Rangipuke. Rangi (sky) puke (hill). I didn't know this on the day I wed in the shadows of a Moreton Bay fig. Under the expansive arms, I signed a document on a little wooden table that the minister thankfully thought to bring to the park, to change my name. Becky Helm/ Rebecca Beardsall.

REGENCY APARTMENTS, 4H/LORNE STREET

Too often our breakfast consists of a filled-roll or scone from a takeaway shop. Today I decide to make scrambled eggs. Bright orange globes rest in the blue glass bowl waiting to be whisked. Creamy yellow butter spreads out in the frying pan. Geoff instructs me that I can't make scrambled eggs in a frying pan. *Can't* rings wrong somehow. I've been making scrambled eggs in a frying pan for years – just like my mother, grandmother, and great-grandmother.

Saucepan on the stove. Staying true to the customs of my new land. Colonial blue plate houses the pillow of fluffy eggs on buttery toast. He puts down his coffee and asks, *Where's the Wattie's spaghetti?*

Canned?

We *can't* eat things from cans, can we?

LIVEWIRE

Our life in Auckland meant long hours sitting within the walls of LiveWire. A small shop with a glass storefront within the Mid City complex, a mix of shops and restaurants, plus the picture theater. LiveWire was right at the top of the escalators on the second floor. It was a prime location as everyone had to walk by to get to the movies.

The front of the shop housed quads of computers surrounded by bright red chairs. These computers were usually packed with people, mainly guys, playing networked computer games like Command & Conquer, Duke Nukem, Quake, Diablo, etc. This was the power of LiveWire. When computers and internet were still emerging into private homes, LiveWire provided a place for groups of people to come together to play multiplayer LAN (local area network) games.

At the back of the shop were the custom-built computer tables that Geoff designed – a half-circle table with three red chairs around a computer set down into a circular table. These were mostly used by travelers to access email and Microsoft Office to create CVs (curriculum vitae). This is usually where I hung out because it was right next to the reception desk where

Geoff or our daytime manager, Carlos, worked the main computer, monitoring everyone's time and managing payments.

Early on, my only reprieve from the testosterone-filled shop was when Carolyn would invite me to go out with her. Carolyn's brother was one of Geoff's first employees, but he moved on to another job by the time I moved to Auckland. These jaunts outside of LiveWire started with shopping trips on a Saturday afternoon or meeting her university friends at the Irish pub around the corner on a Friday night. Eventually, my time with Carolyn would take me into the arts around Auckland, which exposed me to the true joy of living in a city. Growing up in Pennsylvania, we often would go to see shows on Broadway in New York City as part of a bus tour or travel into Philadelphia with school, but I had never before lived in a place where the opera, ballet, and plays were within walking distance.

Each day on my walk from the apartment to LiveWire I would walk past the Civic Theatre, which first opened in 1929, and Aotea Centre, which opened six years before my arrival in Aotearoa New Zealand, both hubs for the arts in Auckland. I attended my first opera and my first professional ballet sitting alongside Carolyn in the plush seats of Aotea Centre. Saturday and Sunday matinees became regular dates with Carolyn. I would take the short walk from Mid City to Aotea.

Our enjoyment of the arts as spectators transitioned to hands-on experience when Carolyn invited me to join her in some classes, from printmaking to pottery, at ArtStation located at 1 Ponsonby Road Grey Lynn. I would get the bus on rainy winter nights to meet Carolyn at the studio inside what used to be the Ponsonby Police Barracks, where we would shape coils of clay into vases or dig our Pfeil linocut tools into grey linoleum. I still have pieces from those classes in my house today, some twenty-five years later, including an etching plate print hanging on the wall of my library and a blue pottery platter that I use whenever we are entertaining guests.

And it was Carolyn who took me shopping for my wedding dress. A dress I never found, a small-town girl shopping in the city looking for a simple white dress while void of style-sense or what looked good on my body type. Even though I went with a blouse and skirt for my outfit, I still wanted to have something to make it special and feel like a wedding. I had stacks of bridal magazines that I borrowed from the library and in one of them there was a model wearing a long flowing sheer scarf around her neck instead of a veil. I loved this look and searched for something like it. Carolyn enlisted the help of her mum to recreate that scarf for me.

UPRIGHT

YOU ARE ON THE RIGHT PATH. TRUST YOUR INSTINCTS AND ALLOW THE UNIVERSE TO PROVIDE.

REVERSED

YOU HAVE A CHOICE AHEAD OF YOU. BE WARY OF THE SHADOW PATH. STOP AND LISTEN TO YOUR INSTINCTS BEFORE MOVING FORWARD.

WHAT RISK?

Passing the plate of chocolate chip cookies to the person next to me, I balance the book and a cookie on my knee while holding onto my mug of coffee. I *don't know if I would call it a risk. She just made a decision and acted on it. For the second part of the question, I don't think I am a person that necessarily takes risks.* I see some gaping mouths, and I lift the cookie to my lips to avoid feeling awkward.

I disagree with you, says Donna. *So, you thinking selling your house in Pennsylvania, packing up your life, driving across the country to Bellingham, a city you've never been to before and without jobs wasn't a risk?*

Well, not really. We made a decision and followed through.

Well, I would consider that a risk, Donna says while the rest of the book club nods in agreement.

Maybe, I shake my head and squint my eyes as if this will help me think about it.

Thankfully someone interjects to answering the original question and I'm left to ponder my risk. The discussion stays on risk, but I'm no longer linking it to the book we are looking at during tonight's book club meeting.

I start looking at the narrative of my life, plots on the map of moments, and realize to many I am a big risk-taker. I move to Aotearoa New Zealand to marry someone I met online. We later leave our amazing life behind in Aotearoa New Zealand to land back in the United States without possessions and only $1000 in our bank account. Later, we leave great careers and a lovely home to move to the Pacific Northwest. I can see how people might see these as rash and risky. However, I never do. Not once did I pause and think, *Wait, a lot could go wrong here.* Have I really thought about all the consequences?

Tracey, my sister-in-law, once said I was very lucky. Things just always worked out for me.

I think about her statement when I'm thinking about risk with a group of women I met only a couple of months ago at my new job. Living in a new city, starting a new life, and never once did I consider it a risk.

During my brother's funeral, the church is in the middle of a series talking about missions, and in large letters behind the pulpit the phrase "Vision to Venture" announces itself back to the congregation. My uncle takes up this theme when talking about my brother. He mentions, *Dwayne was always focused and knew what he wanted. He worked hard to get to where he wanted to be. He believed he would be a farmer from the time he was a little boy, and he had the vision to make it happen on his own.*

I soak in these words. I also consider that my brother only had twenty-five years to reach his vision and in an instant, it was gone.

One afternoon during my lunch break at the bookstore a month before I move to Aotearoa New Zealand, a colleague slurping her soup asks how much older Geoff is to me. I rarely have time for busy-bodies, but I answer, *Fifteen years.*

Oh, goodness, she puts down her spoon and looks at me from across the table. The rest of the people sitting around us turn their attention to our conversation. *Well, you know women live longer than men. He will die long before you.*

Oh yeah, I stab my salad. *Tell that to my sister-in-law. She married someone closer to her age and he died a long time before her. I'm not making my decision based on death. I'm deciding on life. On now. On this moment.*

Sitting in book club and thinking back to that conversation and Tracey's comment about luck, I see that I have made bold decisions that obviously would have made others pause, but you get one life – I always tell myself – live it. If I learned anything from the death of my brother, it is that I should reach for what I want and not wait for life to just happen to me.

I wonder sometimes how my life may have been different had Dwayne not died. Would I have been strong enough to move to Aotearoa New Zealand to marry someone I met online? Would I have stayed in Scotland to be the missionary that everyone wanted me to be? I have a feeling I would have stayed in Pennsylvania for the rest of my life, married some good Mennonite boy, and continued on in a life that wasn't right for me, but what was expected. My brother, in his death, gave me the courage to live life boldly. I owe it to him and to myself to relish in the world and each breath I am able to take.

Is risk part of my method of living? I guess. But aren't we all taking risks each day as we drive on the roads, walk in the woods, fly through the sky in metal tubes? Life is risk; it is just a matter of if you let the weight of it stop you or buoy you.

BYLINE

When I moved to Aotearoa New Zealand, I left behind the start of my college career in creative writing. Still in the infant stages of understanding the writing world, I checked out books on publishing from the Central City Library on Lorne St., a mere minute's walk from our apartment. When Geoff first told me about our new place in Regency Apartments, a relatively new building built in 1995, he never mentioned proximity to the library. However, on our first daytime walk from the apartment to his internet café LiveWire, he pointed it out to me. I stopped and looked back to where we just came from, and I laughed. *I can walk to the library*, I said—a novel idea for a small-town girl. A library with escalators, of all things. Magical.

Drawing on my limited life experience to this point in time – which consisted of working in bookstores and preschools – I moved momentarily away from adult fiction to trying my hand at children's books. I was twenty-one when I shifted my focus to writing; before that, I worked as a preschool teacher in Pennsylvania and Montana. Taking the advice from the author on publishing books, I looked into submitting work to magazines. I submitted an article on party ideas for preschoolers to *Little Treasures*, a parenting magazine in Aotearoa New

Zealand. To my utter shock and delight, they accepted and published my story—my first byline.

Every day for a week on my walk to our internet café, I would stop by Whitcoulls to pick up a copy of Little Treasures and flip to the same page. Rebecca Helm – my new/old name in print.

Rebecca Helm is a freelance writer living in Auckland and has been a pre-school teacher.

I wrote a few more articles for *Little Treasures*; then, they asked me to help with some resources from the internet for a feature story. Geoff's internet café provided the perfect space for this. While individuals still had to contend with dial-up in their homes, I had the luxury of DSL (digital subscriber line), high-speed internet, at my fingertips. I continued in this role for *Little Treasures* for two more years. However, this request from the editor at *Little Treasures* prompted me to think about other opportunities.

When I read that the Aotearoa New Zealand-based women's magazine *More* merged with the Australian-based *SHE*, I saw my moment. I reached out to the new editor, Jane Binsley, and pitched my idea of an internet column to talk about trends online for the newly merged magazine. She contacted me for an interview scheduled for the day we got back from our trip around the middle of the North Island with a couple of friends. A journey that created memories of a geothermal champagne pool, boiling mud, glow worms. It would also account for the scar above my right eye after the four of us decided to link legs down the waterslide like we were twelve-year-olds. High up in the twisting slide, when Geoff finally screamed, *Let go*, I flipped into the air, leaving the slide altogether. By some luck, I landed back into the bright blue, plastic funnel of death. Swished into the shallow pool below with blood gushing from my eyebrow, I stood up, covered my face, and announced, *I nearly died up there.* I spent the rest of the night in our cabin with a flannel on my head, debating stitches.

I walked into the office of *SHE & More* hoping my glasses frame covered up my second right eyebrow, the gnarly scab that formed from my altercation with the waterslide. I laughed it off as I pulled my portfolio out of the leather satchel Geoff bought me for my first Aotearoa New Zealand job interview. I landed the column. I like to think the scab had something to do with it, a visible sign that I had Aotearoa New Zealand grit. I could tackle waterslides and live to tell the tale, and I was bold enough not to cancel my appointment to pitch an innovative idea because I looked like a monster. Aotearoa New Zealand is the land of rugby, after all, so what's a few scars and scabs?

I danced around the apartment when I heard from *SHE & More,* my first actual column with a real monthly deadline. I finally had my own job, a writing job, outside of working for Geoff's business. My baby steps towards a career in writing.

I was settling into a new city, a new country, a new name. I was part of *SHE & More,* the glossy that won Best Magazine Launch by the Magazine Publishers' Association in 1997, and it was a finalist in the 198 Best News-Stand Magazine category at the Qantas Media Awards.

HUSBAND

Summer sun rests high in the sky.
    Our car hurtles down Mount Ruapehu.
    The Tongariro National Park landscape is brown and barren. Carolyn fails to tell us she is worried about not having enough petrol to get back to town. She allows the car to coast. Down. Picking up speed turn after turn. Taking in the expansive views from the backseat. Everything is moving too fast. I hear Carolyn pull the handbrake. She strains to lift it. It only just holds. We skid into a pull off with nothing in front of us but the bluest of skies.
    Tires hit gravel. I grab Geoff's hand. The car shudders to a stop. I feel death reach out. Fingers swiping by my shoulder in a fleeting attempt.
    Smoke and searing brakes. The only souls on the side of a volcano. I want to panic. I need to cry. I look to my husband, my husband – a term still trying to sink its way into me.

WHAT DO YOU SEE?

Perhaps it was August or September 1997. I know it was late winter, or early spring, because of the constant rain and still short hours of daylight. Not that we saw much daylight. In general, much of the time we worked until 1 a.m. and slept in until 10 a.m., giving us a few hours in the sunlight before being tucked back into the shop in Mid City. I never realized how much I missed windows that faced the outside world until I worked in the Internet Lounge – the glass front and door opened out into the mall. Fluorescent lights gave the sense of constant day, but it could be raining, sunny, night, or day. We never knew. Occasionally, we had days off or an evening away from work when we hired a few more people to help support the daily running of the shop. One such occasion was the winter we took a class at a spiritual center in Auckland.

We have had debates as to where this center was located. Geoff insists we took the motorcycle, and it was on the North Shore. I thought we took the bus, which means it was on a loop close to the city center. We also cannot remember the name of the place, nor how we heard about it. I have a feeling it was a customer that came into LiveWire that invited us. We often had customers invite us to things – the dancers, singers, and musicians from *Riverdance* used to come into LiveWire; they gave us tickets to a performance and had everyone sign the souvenir program. We often had the cast of *Xena* and *Hercules* in to use email. At one point, a member from one of America's Cup teams was a regular, and she invited me to a studio in Devonport on Sunday mornings to experience NIA, a dance, martial arts-based exercise, and healing program. So, it is entirely possible that we were invited to join a spiritual awakening class by a regular or only for a season/while-our-team/cast/troupe-is-in-the-city type customer.

We attended this class each week for several months. I often made Geoff sit in the back with me. I wasn't quite ready to throw myself fully into this world. Geoff was way more open to the mystical than I was. The first night we talked about the third eye and witnessing. The instructor had someone sit on a wooden stool at the front of the class. Then she encouraged us to see with our third eye. *What do you see?* she asked us with an expectant smile on her face. I looked at her and then at the person on the stool. I saw the typical white glow I've been seeing around people most of my life. I often saw this glow around people at the pulpit at church, the lectern at school, on stage even. It usually required a blank wall behind them for me to see it, and I thought it was just the play of light (and it still might be that). However, when people started talking about light and shadow in this room, I looked more closely at the glow around people that was as familiar to me as sitting in a pew at church.

To engage the third eye, unfocus your eyes, or close your eyes, and pull the energy toward the center of your forehead just above your nose, said the instructor. I tried to do as she suggested, but it started to give me a headache. I opened my eyes, looking still in the direction of the person on the stool at the front of the room and noticed a tall shadow standing on her left, my right. I quickly shook my head, and it was gone. *My imagination*, I told myself. The power of suggestion. I listened to the people in the room start sharing – colors, guides, people. I leaned over and whispered to Geoff, *Do you see anything?*

No, he responded.

Me neither, I said.

We would repeat this exercise of a classmate sitting in front and sharing what we saw every meeting. The instructor would start the class by teaching us different ways to awake spiritually and then would ask for someone to join her at the front of the room. It would almost be the last session when she asked, *Who hasn't been up front yet?* And it felt as if the whole room turned and looked at me. I really didn't want to go up there. I didn't want to hear what they saw. I wanted to remain in my land of denial. I didn't want to believe any of this was real. I was just going through the motions and attending a class with Geoff, a mere activity for us to do together in a world usually revolving around work, sleeping, and eating. My Mennonite upbringing didn't provide the space for intense spiritual spaces even within the so-called Christian church. I remember when I first experienced people speaking in tongues when I lived in Scotland; when I returned home and questioned what I saw with my pastor, he told me that the spiritual gifts of the Bible were for a particular time and they were no longer needed or a part of our time. Basically, ignore those passages in the Bible, they aren't meant for us. So here I was, in the spiritual center, being pushed to see and believe something that Becky would deny.

I shuffled around the chairs and bodies, moving from the very back of the room to the front. I have no record of this. I'm sure there were some notes taken, but I most likely destroyed them as I often did with anything connected to spirituality beyond the church's teaching. I'd go through phases of stress about having non-church things in my house, and I'd throw them out. But I do remember they said they saw a man and a woman supporting me. They said I was spiritually connected.

I sat there with a forced smile on my face just waiting for

it to be over. I walked back to my seat with my head bowed and shoulders slumped. I didn't know what to do with what I heard. Part of me really wanted to believe it, but I was too scared. Too afraid to open myself up to the unknown.

Oddly enough, I didn't write much about my experiences from these classes in my journal at the time. Not that I wrote much in a journal when I lived in Aotearoa New Zealand – maybe once or twice a month. Most of my journal from that time is filled with prayers to God to help me. To provide me with friends. To help me feel connected to my new life as wife and Kiwi. The only mention of this class: "Did mirror work – saw older lady with a round face (reminded me of a wise one from stories) . . . Also, great revelations from class – I was happiest and more on level with higher-self when connected to the arts. Connected in spiritual matters. More meditation." More meditation, an instruction I often hear.

***

At this spiritual center, we would also talk to the director. David, Daniel, Gary. I can't remember his name, but I do remember two of the things he said to us. He looked down at the cards in front of him and told us we had or would have two children. A boy and a girl. I heard this later from a clairvoyant when I was still on my quest about kids. I knew going in that Geoff didn't want kids, and at the time, I didn't want any either. But that didn't stop me from asking any future-seeing voice if I would have children. (I actually don't think I would have ever been able to carry a child to term, let alone get pregnant. I have PCOS, which often comes with infertility). We said, *No, we don't have kids*. Geoff said, *I have a son*. We never clearly understood what all these spiritually connected people saw about a boy and a girl. It may have been our grandchildren.

Maybe even Geoff's son and our daughter-in-law, or maybe the children we would have had together had we taken that life path.

However, the other thing the director of the Spiritual Centre said has stayed with me my whole life. He looked directly at me and told me I had a direct connection to the spirit world. *You are very connected. Do you ever hear a buzzing in your ear?*

I looked at him and slowly nodded.

That's the spirit world trying to communicate with you. You need to learn to open yourself up to hear.

That was the last thing I wanted to do. I immediately wanted to leave the room. It felt like it was closing in on me. I didn't want this. *I didn't ask for this. Why me?* It felt like a burden to just know that it was more than just an annoying buzzing in my ear.

It freaked me out because it explained some unexplainable moment in my life. I have a clear memory of playing Barbies in my childhood friend Sherri's bedroom in their house on Cherry Road. I heard a man's voice. It was slow, very slow. At the time, I thought it sounded thick like molasses, *I'm gonna do it.* I remember looking around the room and still hearing the voice, but the only other person in the room was Sherri, sitting down on the floor putting a dress on her Barbie. I shook my body as if to get it off me, and sat down next to her, and started talking loudly to stop the voice in my head. I heard that voice a few more times in that house and never heard it again when visiting Sherri when they moved from that house to Richlandtown.

***

That's the spirit world trying to communicate with you. Just open yourself up and listen, he said.

Nope. That was not going to happen. The next time I heard ringing in my ears, I said out loud, *No, I don't want you talking to me. Go away.* I repeated this every time it happened. Until one day, I asked, *What?*

No reply came, but the spirit world knew I was opening.

Sitting in the transitional zone between the spirit and physical worlds provides the space for communication. Ringing in the ears is said to be a sign of a person's ability to balance the two worlds. If a person has this experience, they may be a clairaudience – hearing beyond, or clear hearing. The person with this spiritual gift tends to be more intuitive and sensitive to all sounds. I seem to always be the person in the room saying, *Do you hear that?* And I receive blank stares in response as people strain to hear and then shake their heads no.

A spiritual awakening happens when the vibrations lift energy into a higher path of knowing. Some spiritual experts believe a ringing in the ear is, in essence, hearing the sound of creation taking place. And since creation is happening continually, it is a wonder someone with this ability wouldn't go insane with all that buzzing noise.

Ringing in the ears can even be linked to earthly transformations like new, full moons or eclipses. It seems the spiritual and earthly possibilities are endless, and people continue to try to figure out how these messages come and why they appear at certain times.

In researching this experience, I found a plethora of information but no real answers. I learn that if the clairaudience is out of balance or going through a spiritual transformation, the pitch may be higher. The emotional connection to the tonal shift is vital to home in on what the spirit world is trying to tell you. Recently I read that the tone and ear matters, adding another stress into my life. I pause, thinking right or left, high or low. Then I try to remember what I read. Is it high-pitched ringing in the right ear means exciting news and good tidings, or is it the left? Low-pitched – is that a warning? How do I determine if it is high or low? High or low according to whose ears?

Ringing ears, of course, can also mean a sign or nerve damage or hearing loss. So, there is that to consider. There is a real health concern with ear ringing. Tinnitus, the medical term for ringing in the ears, is also linked to hypothyroidism and Hashimoto's disease, which I was diagnosed with in my late twenties. This could also explain it, or is Tinnitus merely a medical way of trying to explain the unexplainable?

***

Saturday night is my special night of the week because I can spend the night reading or writing without the concern of getting to bed at a decent hour. I'm a converted night owl. Given to my own devices, I would stay up and create all night long, but the working world demands a different schedule, which means I must stay on a strict cycle of hours of sleep and waking. If I get this too messed up over a vacation or even just the weekend, it can alter my energy for a whole work week. So even though I allow myself longer nights on Fridays and Saturdays it still means I'm in bed by midnight.

This Saturday is no different. We start a movie around 8 p.m., wandering upstairs around 10 o'clock. We then both start our nightly rituals, which include things like checking emails, brushing teeth, reading, writing. Geoff and I each have our own system and timing. We hover around each other, never getting in each other's way. The cat going in and out of the office and bedroom, our nightly dance. She follows me around, waiting for me to settle into bed so she can hop up and sit down next to me. This motion of me pulling the covers over my legs and the cat jumping on the bed is a sign to us both that rest is coming.

Eventually, the bedside lamps are extinguished, and we all settle down into the covers and pillows. Tonight, the bedroom window is ajar, providing fresh, crisp autumn air. This gentle breeze causes me to snuggle down into the covers. I'm a side sleeper. My childhood through early adult years I slept on my stomach, but with a flirtation of side sleeping. By thirty, my back no longer allowed for nights of stomach sleeping. Bodies have a way of telling us how to behave. Tonight, I'm on my right side, facing the middle of the bed and Geoffrey. The cat is curled into a ball by my feet. I nuzzle my head into my pillow and welcome the blissful late-night sleep. A well-desired rest after a long day of yoga, farmer's market CSA collection, weekly meal prep, writing. I hear Geoff move into a deeper sleep as his breathing changes. My eyes heavy and sleep welcoming in the whispers of the night. I'm moving to the in-between place. Space between awake and dreaming.

My foot got caught in my pants. I tripped.

My eyes spring open. Wide awake now, I try to reconcile the male voice I just heard. Who was it? I lie still, trying to determine if there is someone in the room. Who just whispered into my ear? My heart is racing. I've never heard a voice so clear.

I take a few deep breaths. Calming myself down. Was that Dwayne? No one was around when he fell into the mixer. We don't know how it happened. Just that it did. Now I wonder was that him speaking to me. Was he trying to explain his accident to me?

I don't know. It is hours before I feel I am able to let the voice go and to drift back to sleep.

First thing in the morning, I tell Geoff what I heard. This is not something I can keep inside. What could it mean?

I tripped.

***

That's the spirit world trying to communicate with you. Just open yourself up and listen, he said.

Much later, I realized that there was nothing to be afraid of when I open myself up to more spiritual elements beyond what I understand. As a kid, my favorite Bible story was when Samuel heard the Lord call to him in the night. I think I was drawn to this story because it helped me, as a child, to put a frame around various experiences I had but couldn't explain. Before I was willing to believe there was more voices to be heard, I followed Eli's advice to Samuel: "So Eli told Samuel, 'Go and lie down, and if he calls you, say, "Speak, Lord, for your servant is listening."'"

PIHA

The alarm called out into the darkness of morning. Groggy, we gathered clothing and shuffled towards the elevator. We had a rental car for once but had to move it before the city parking enforcement hours started. A long journey to Taumarunui, a first trip beyond the cocooning of the city, took us to the threshold of Geoff's parents' door. They followed a strict British understanding of tea. Geoff and I slept in old twin beds, each with our own hot water bottle. That was all the warmth to fend off the spring frost in Taumarunui.

    The street cleaner turned the corner just as the automatic glass doors thrust us into a whoosh of cool air. We followed the street cleaner around the corner, as if the song of the brushes beckoned. We walked up Wyndham to the car – a little white Toyota hatchback. We still had a few hours before the rental shop opened. Geoff decided we would go to Piha.

    We both yawned as Geoff started the car and eased it out of the parking space. The street quiet; just the two of us moved through the dawn to Piha. I envisioned glorious golden sand and turquoise waves reaching out, welcoming us into their embrace.

    We arrived at the west coast beach, my first visit to black sand. We realized quickly that we didn't grab enough clothing to protect us from the morning sea air still fierce from its night rituals. The feathery hands of toetoe waved a welcome as we walked to the beach. Lion Rock, large and looming, told the tale of strength and persistence – stood proud on the beach laughing at the sea.

Our courtship started in the snow-blanketed hills of Pennsylvania. Here on Aotearoa New Zealand shores, I wanted to run and dance in the waves, but the cold kept me clinging to Geoff. He wrapped his arm around me and kissed me on the forehead.

Geoff took me to the ocean and showed Rebecca the heart of where she lived.

UPRIGHT

EVERYTHING IS IN FRONT OF YOU. THE UNIVERSE IS OPENING UP OPPORTUNITIES AND THIS IS YOUR CHANCE TO EXPAND AND EXPLORE. BOLDLY STEP FORWARD.

EDGE OF THE WORLD

REVERSED

THE HORIZON IS AHEAD OF YOU, BUT THIS IS NOT THE TIME TO MOVE FORWARD. INSTEAD, THE UNIVERSE IS ASKING YOU TO REST AND WAIT FOR THE SEA OF ABUNDANCE AND PEACE TO COME TO YOU.

THAT'S AN R

Determined to continue to find my place in the city, I decided to take a French class at AUT – Auckland University of Technology, formerly Auckland Institute of Technology. It seemed like a logical step since I love going to school, but I wasn't quite ready to start another degree in Auckland. On the first day of my French class, we were handed a worksheet to provide details about our French language experiences and our expectations for the course. I started to pen my name on the name line by writing an R with a flourish. Robin, our instructor, commented, *Now that is a well-practiced R*. She smiled down at me while she handed the worksheet to the classmate next to me. I glanced over at the tall, blonde woman on my right looking at me and my R. Little did either of them know that it was only recently that I started to go by the name Rebecca and flicking my wrist just so to create my signature R.

    I made a lifelong friend in this French class – the tall blonde sitting next to me. Kerstin was from Germany and also new to Auckland. We would take classes together from February – June 1998. And then venture into aqua aerobics while continuing our French lessons via *French in Action* VHS tapes.

MOLASSES

I'm alone in our apartment. Windows open out to the noise of the city on Friday night. I call Geoff at work and ask where I can buy molasses.

Molasses? That's cattle food.

No, it's not. I want to make cupcakes. Revulsion rings through the receiver.

I page through my Mennonite cookbook. Its list of ingredients, now exotic, tempts me. I leave my safe zone to join the stream of people walking Queen Street. At the corner dairy, I seek the labels of my childhood – names that force my German tongue to its roots. Amongst a sea of Wattie's products, I spy a glass bottle, slightly dusty, which brings promise and memories swirling. I open the bottle at home with hopes of sugary, earthy goodness. Spoon dips slowly into the thick, brown-black syrup. Catching the expanding string on my finger, I lift it to my lips. My longing mislaid in bitterness.

He arrives home and sees the open bottle of molasses.

Did you make cupcakes?

No, that stuff is disgusting.

Geoff shakes his head in that I-told-you-so tone. I'm stuck eating pavlova with bright yellow, larvae-like seeds of passion fruit.

WITH LOVE, CASSEROLE
(AKA, TWENTY-THREE-YEAR-OLD BECOMES STEPMUM TO A TEENAGER)

The hard-formed plastic table, the kind only found in amusement parks and fast-food restaurants, still had the previous occupants' residue – bread crumbs, moisture rings, and greasy, salty fingerprints. We stared at each other and waited for someone to talk. I looked beyond Reece to the stream of bodies that progressed down Queen Street. In the city, Friday night turned the streets into a party, which grew louder, angrier, and sillier as the alcohol started its work in bloodstreams. The night was still early, and the laughter and shouts outside the Wendy's seemed like any other night in Auckland. Friday. What a dumb night to force a teenager to work on homework, Rebecca. I volunteered for this when Kathie called Geoff to say Reece, their sixteen-year-old, was struggling at school. I'd tutored before and prided myself on working with teenagers, having been oh-so-recently a teenager myself. Reece glared back at me from under his red-dyed, long in front, skater hair. His eyes revealed anger (or was it loathing) at me, his soon to be step-mum.

    I watched Reece pull two books and a mixture of crumpled paper out of his backpack. Our first time alone together. Geoff was across the street at work. As Reece and I walked out the glass door to head to Wendy's, Geoff winked at me. I couldn't decide if the wink was for good luck or thanks. I smoothed out the papers. Missed assignments. Late papers. Blank math homework sheets. *Reece, you can do this, but you need to get organized first.* This is a mess, I waved my hand over the mass of multi-colored papers on the plastic table. In response, I received a slow blink and a nod. Progress? I grabbed the paper on the top of the pile. *Okay, let's start with this math assignment. When is this one due?* I tilted my head and waited. Answer: shrug. I clasped my hands and rested them on my chin. I waited. Finally, a mumble emerged. It sounded like Monday. *Right. Let's look at all of your assignments and write down the due dates. It will help us plan.* I had bought a little blue spiral notebook at Woolworth's earlier in the day just for this moment. I started to print each task and date. I drew a line at the bottom. *Have your mum sign off on this when you've completed each one. It will help you stay accountable.* Pursed-lipped snarl.

I should have known he would forge his mother's signature. But I wasn't prepared for the anger that it released inside me.

***

A year of weekend visits with Reece made my clean apartment smell like a locker room. Often, multiple boys slept in our living room. One morning we woke to stolen CDs, a sweep of plastic spines to hide the holes. Snot oozed down the side of my meticulously scrubbed sink. Wet towels left on beds every-single-time. Sullen non-verbal replies. *He is your son. You need to talk to him.*

It took a year for me to give up on the notion of step-mum finally. Reece already had a mum. He didn't need me, but I needed to find a way to make him feel welcome and loved in our home.

I grew up Mennonite, where hospitality meant food. And by food, I don't mean gourmet morsels. I mean stick-to-the-ribs, comfort food. Church gatherings warranted eight six-foot-long tables weighed down by multiple colored casserole dishes. White plastic tablecloths carefully placed on the table, but the only evidence of its existence was the three-inch overhang on the side. Every spot filled with trays of lasagna, baked ziti, macaroni and cheese. Bowls of potato salad, macaroni salad, and the latest trend in Jell-O salads. Yellow potato buns rested by trays of cheese and lunchmeats followed by glass dishes of mustard, mayo, and pickle relish. Eggs – egg salad finger sandwiches, deviled eggs, pickled red beet eggs, quiches filled full of garden-fresh vegetables.

Then there were four six-foot tables filled with desserts. Whoopie pies, shoo-fly pie, cream puffs, cupcakes, twenty different varieties of chocolate cake, cookies, cheese pie, cheesecake, angel food cake, sour cream pound cake, carrot cake, fruit pies.

When I decided to return to my understanding of hospitality, I looked to my mom. I had watched her for years make food for weddings, funerals, church gatherings, progressive dinners. Baking – any Mennonite kid could do that. Baking was in our blood. Cakes, pies, cookies.

Cooking, on the other hand, took a different type of skill.

Geoff and I ate out most of the time because of our crazy work schedule, but I wanted to make meals when Reece came on the weekends. I called Mom and asked her to fax me some recipes. Specifically, I asked for Dad's meatloaf, her parmesan crusted chicken, and Nana's ham and potato casserole recipes. And my favorite macaroni and cheese recipe copied from a *Betty Crocker Cookbook*... or was it *Better Homes and Gardens*? A recipe from the 70s, the copied page with dark spots of spilled liquids. I lived in a land where half the brands and ingredients I grew up with didn't exist, but mac and cheese components are easy to find anywhere.

I never realized how long it took to make homemade macaroni and cheese. Since I was old enough to use the stove, I was handed a box of Kraft mac and cheese. I put on my denim apron and tackled Mom's recipe.

Long slivers of cheese tumbled down from the grater as the water started to rumble on the stove. Large elbow noodles clattered their way into the pot as I marveled at their odd size – they were larger than the noodles we had in Pennsylvania. My face reddened from the pasta water steam as I whisked the creamy, golden yellow butter and flour together. I stood and stirred the white sauce for what seemed like hours. I would later learn to call it Béchamel sauce.

Reece and Geoff beamed as I walked the white casserole dish to the small, dark wood table I bought when we moved to Queen Street. Large spoonfuls of cheesy noodles mounded onto plates. Silence. Then, *This is good.* I sat with my hands clasped on the table and exhaled.

SWALLOWED WHOLE

A time in the world before Skype, digital photos, social media, I had to wait for photographs to arrive in the mail, a minimum of ten days to travel from Quakertown to Auckland. Most of my friends and family didn't have the internet at home. Instead, they used work computers when they could spare a moment. Screaming fax machines with rolls of paper inching out a message were our form of instant communication.

My homesickness swallowed me whole when we went back to Pennsylvania for Christmas. We spent six weeks of the holidays with my family and friends in Pennsylvania, and on the long flight back to Aotearoa New Zealand, Geoff and I started talking about moving back to the USA for a while. The plan was five years. That would mean five years in NZ and five years in the US; we lived in Pennsylvania for nine years. Nine long years. Until we both couldn't handle the East Coast anymore.

Aotearoa New Zealand had just started to sink into me when we left. My excitement of being home with my family and friends would delay my mourning, but I would realize what exactly I turned my back on in the South Pacific when it hit. When I finally discovered myself in my early thirties,

I realized that I already had a place that held me. It wasn't where I was raised. It was where I was transplanted.

Would it ever open its arms to me? Would I be welcomed into the Kiwi fold again, or was my departure my last chance to claim that name?

18 OCTOBER 1999

We are on the cusp of leaving Aotearoa New Zealand. On the recommendation of Geoff's sister, we are sitting in the lounge of a clairvoyant's house in Tauranga. One by one, we go into her study for our reading. I am skeptical and do my best not to give anything away. The clairvoyant starts recording on a cassette tape. The cassette has since been destroyed. This happened on one of my frantic, Christian guilt-ridden rampages. I regret it. She sees an older man from my mother's side. She asks if my grandfather is still living. He is – happily enjoying his life and rose gardens in Collegeville, Pennsylvania. She can't seem to shake the connection. I have no idea who she is talking about. It is someone that connected to me when I was younger from my mother's side. I shrug, and she moves on. Thinking about this on the drive back to Auckland. I started to wonder if the man was someone connected to Pop-pop. When I asked Mom about any men on Pop-pop's side of the family that I might be connected to, she mentioned Pop-pop's business partner, Joe, from McConnell & Gottshall Electric Appliance. Mom said Joe loved seeing me in the store and often asked about me.

The clairvoyant takes me through things coming my way: gardens, two children (a boy and a girl), success in the future.

She tells me she sees a fluffy cat. It is an old soul, and it is connected to me. *A very fluffy cat,* she keeps saying over and over. This prediction came true. My cat Myrtle who we adopted in 2007, a fluffy, old soul British Shorthair, would see me through some challenging moments in my life. She turns off the tape and informs me that Geoff is not my soulmate, but that this is okay because my soulmate is not here in this cycle. However, we will have a very rocky relationship, she tells me. *It will be difficult, and you will have significant ups and downs.* Thankfully, this did not come to pass, or at least not in the way I took her meaning. It could simply have been that I am more stoic and practical than she realized. Life is life is life. It comes with joys and sadness. I learned that lesson early on when my brother Dwayne died.

Turning the tape back on, she starts to talk about my health. I watch her shoulders slump as she reaches for her neck. *You hold so much on your shoulders. You keep your tension around your neck, spanning out into your shoulders.* She tilts her head as if to release the feeling of the constant tightness in my body I am prone to ignore. Still holding her neck, she starts to press against it. I watch her fingers dig into her flesh, *Your metabolism is so slow. Slow – to the point it is nonexistent. Walking. Walking will help this.* Years later, I realize she predicted my thyroid disease, Hashimoto's, well before the doctors did, even though I saw many medical professionals about not feeling well and living in a state of debilitating exhaustion. I took her comment on walking to heart. I started walking daily in 2003 and never stopped.

She then asks if I have any questions. I ask about Dwayne's widow, Tracey. My skepticism waiting to see what she would say. To my surprise, she says, *I see Tracey far away. Across a lot of water.* Accurate. Tracey is in Pennsylvania. I ask if she is okay, which the clairvoyant confirms. I ask a few more basic, non-important questions. Then I casually ask, *Anything about Dwayne?* She smiles and says, *He was wondering when you were going to ask for him.* And I lose it. Bawling with snot running down my face, I listen to her relay his messages to me. I can see she is trying to work out the emotional reaction. I'm sure most people come in wanting to hear from dead loved ones, and I so casually asked about my dead brother. He tells me there was no pain in this death. I sob. He tells me that he is with me and is proud of me. He likes when we get to throw football together in my dreams. I reach for the tissue box she hands me. Later in the day, I will write in my journal about this moment. Out of all she told me, the only thing I wrote about was my brother: "I cried, and I am still crying. I just miss him so much. It has been hard for me living here without him – life may move on, but deep inside me I have an empty place in me. Dwayne, please know that I love you so very much. And you are such a wonderful spirit, and love, kindness are what makes you so beautiful. I miss you. I wish you could be here and share this life with me. I will look after Mom and Daddy… and even Amanda. We miss you so very much."

That day, I became a believer. I couldn't explain it. It wasn't just because I wanted to believe it, but I have no idea how she knew those things unless she was really communicating with my brother. I would waver back and forth in my belief in the afterlife and the larger connection of life, energy, and light surrounding us. It clashed with all my teachings as a child. I will dismiss this experience as occult in years from this moment in Tauranga as the last throes of the Christianity I knew slides away from me. I will start to move into myself. To become fully Rebecca as I embrace the true spiritual side of myself. This moment was a watershed occasion. The curtain falling away.

UPRIGHT

A SECRET HAS BEEN REVEALED.
YOU HAVE ALL THE INFORMATION YOU NEED TO MOVE FORWARD.

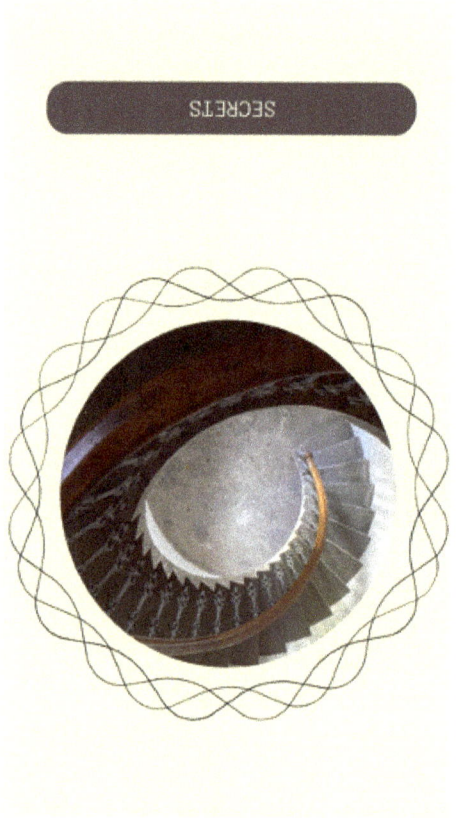

REVERSED

ALL IS NOT WHAT IT SEEMS. THE INSIGHTS ARE HIDDEN FROM YOU RIGHT NOW. TAKE TIME TO SEEK OUT THE ANSWERS AND ASK SOURCE FOR GUIDANCE.

SECTION II

"Who are you?" said the Caterpillar. This was not an encouraging opening for a conversation.

Alice replied, rather shyly, "I, I hardly know, Sir, just at present, at least I know who I was when I got up this morning, but I think I must have been changed several times since then."

**— LEWIS CARROLL,
ALICE'S ADVENTURES IN WONDERLAND (1865)**

FIRST RETURN

Eleven years since we left Aotearoa New Zealand for an adventure and to build our life together in the United States, and we are now on a plane returning to Auckland. A lot has happened in eleven years that we have only witnessed via letters, emails, phone calls, and Skype video chats. Mum and Dad moved from Taumarunui to Dannevirke. Clive, Geoff's brother, moved from Ngāruawāhia to Pirongia, blending his family with Steph's, who will become my sister-in-law in 2015 and an instant friend on our meeting the day before Reece's wedding. Reece is no longer a teenager, but a successful business owner, a father of a nineteen-month-old, and a day away from his wedding. We have new family members to meet as our already blended family is about to join with Reece's wife Renee's family, and new homes to visit in Massey, Pirongia, and Dannevirke – no one has remained in the home they were in when we left at the dawn of the new millennium.

We fly into the city we once called home during the dawning of the day. Outside the plane window below the thick black sky, there is a hint of blue with a small sliver of yellow-orange welcoming in the day. A long, thin cloud rests ever so gently between where the yellow meets the orange sky, and I whisper, *Aotearoa*, Land of the long white cloud. Eleven years and the first time back since we left our life in Auckland. At this point in my life, I have learned the loss of what we left behind. I mourned and continue to mourn what could have been had we stayed because it was me and my homesickness that took us away from the South Pacific. And in so many ways, I reverted to my old self in Pennsylvania. By the time of this trip, we have lived in Bellingham, Washington, on the west coast of the USA for five months, and I am slowly moving more completely into myself.

It is not lost on me that I am returning to Aotearoa New Zealand, in the same month that we got married, and I am the exact age Geoff was at our wedding.

Now looking back at that date and my solar return for 2011, I realize that Saturn was square to my nodes, which is a crossroads where one must acknowledge the past to move into the future, and this is when the future reflects the past, which is ahead – a spiral. My soul's evolutionary journey. My second Lunar nodes return. A time to see what to embrace and what to release. An alignment on purpose and power. This is the start of my separating from my past and acknowledging who I really am by no longer allowing others to define me. Transformation moving me towards growth. And the start of my second transformation into myself begins again when we return to us where we started in Aotearoa New Zealand. Without realizing it, this return reunites me with a self I left behind. She was waiting patiently amongst the trees in Albert Park, the girl I allowed to be defined by someone else, who gave up herself to fit into a concept of marriage that wasn't her own but what she was raised to believe marriage looked like, and I found her again on our last day, our last hours in Auckland before we leave for Bellingham.

MY PLACE IN THE SPIRAL

As I go about my daily life in Auckland, I often walk into a photograph in progress. For the most part, the posing is obvious, and I am able to maneuver around the tourists. But sometimes they stop abruptly in the middle of the footpath, causing all of us trying to get to and from work to stop and wait. Sometimes we get the universal hand wave to let us know it is safe to continue on, or we wait for the camera to lower before we walk on. I often wonder how many photo albums around the globe contain my image.

I live in one of the tourist capitals of the South Pacific. A day does not go by when I'm not asked to take a photo or stop as a photo is being taken. Smiles beaming as they try to portray their excitement, so they can remember the vacation and how they felt being in the land down under.

Auckland is a beautiful city, and Aotearoa is a gorgeous country. I can understand their desire to capture it. I'm thankful for the people who take photos of the place where I live because I haven't taken the time to stop and see my city through a camera lens. Oh, I have some pictures of when my parents came to visit, but mainly the photos are outside the city when we ventured to some exotic place like Rotorua, Taupo, or Paihia.

The bright blue waters of Waitematā Harbour highlight the City of Sails. Camera lenses focus on the CBD as the sunlight glints off the buildings. I am on the ferry heading to Devonport and I look back at the city; watch people pose on the boat with the Auckland skyline behind them. The Sky Tower stands tall like a proud kauri tree. And people continue to aim their cameras at this focal point of the skyline. Snapping photos which will end up in a vacation album somewhere; they will look fondly at it and remember their time spent in Aotearoa New Zealand.

The Sky Tower isn't just a focal point in a photo for me – it indicates home. An easy marker, like a red pin on a map, to show us home. Our apartment is about 400 meters away from the Sky Tower. I use the tower as a way to direct people to our apartment. If you know where the Tower is, you know how to get to our home.

***

It has been years since we lived in that apartment, and many years since we lived in Aotearoa New Zealand; however, even today, once again heading to Devonport, looking back from the Fullers ferry at the city I call home, I feel a sense of groundedness knowing that the Tower points to a place I lived. It exists. Is still a part of me.

From the Sky Tower, I can follow the outline of the buildings until I see where our apartment stands. The mapping of place confirms that I know this city. I have intimate knowledge of this place that the people who just arrived and snap photos can never know.

They can't call this place home. They might hear me with my reverted American accent and think I'm a tourist too, but my vowels once had the Kiwi twang, and I once walked Queen

Street to go home.

    I am here. I once was here. I will return here. The here always remains.

MEASURED IN COFFEE CUPS

We moved away from Auckland at the dawn of the millennium, and it would take us almost eleven years to return. I feel unsure of my place here – Aotearoa, this blended family. We are here for Reece's wedding. It is 6 a.m. on November 11, 2011. I am nervous as we wait for Reece to pick us up from the airport and drive us down to Vilagrad in Ōhaupō.

My anxiety is ramping up as we sit in a nearly empty arrival lounge. I tend to be a nervous traveler, and Geoff is a great counterbalance for me. He understands my tendency to check the passports, tickets, and wallet multiple times throughout the journey. We create a system where he watches me check it all and put it in my carry-on, so when I get anxious, he tells me, *They are safely in the bag. I watched you put them there.*

But this is a different kind of anxiety. We have arrived, which is usually when I am able to relax, but today I'm worried about all the people we are about to meet. Geoff, noticing my sudden silence, asks if I want a coffee, something to do, I suppose. But I am only able to shake my head no as the enormity of being in Auckland after eleven years slowly sinks in. Geoff returns moments later with a tiny cup of coffee, *I forgot how to order coffee here. It is all different. Long Blacks. Flat Whites. A flat white sounded familiar, so that's what I got.*

Flat white, I repeat. The two words bounce around, trying to find the spot to slip into the corresponding part of my memory. *I think I used to like those.* I reach my hand up for the cup in his hand and take a sip. My eyes close and I'm transported to the scattering of cafes around the city where we used to go to for lunch or a quick break from work. *I remember*, I say, handing the cup back to Geoff as we both see Reece at the same moment bounding into the airport taking the long strides his tall frame allows him to do, propelling him towards his dad.

An awkward reunion of handshakes morphing into hugs and nervous laughter. The anticipation broken we are now able to settle into this new space of being together again.

We miss the birth of our first grandchild nineteen months before. I receive the news of his arrival while sitting in my little cubicle in the basement of Dooling Hall at DeSales University, waiting for a student to arrive for their final EN104 paper conference. I shout the news out to the other professors in the room. *A boy!* Jet. I go into full Grammie mode and shower Jet with clothing and gifts – many boxes shipped around the world. We watch him grow via Skype calls, Facebook video posts, and photos. Yet we have never met him in person.

Just before our arrival back in Aotearoa New Zealand, Renee mentions she is concerned Jet might be scared of us, the people from the screen now in real life. Renee decides to meet us at the airport with Jet to ease him into our acquaintance. We decide it will be best to all join up together in a café. After our welcome from Reece, we gather our bags and follow him through the airport.

We ride the escalators up to a dimly lit space filled with tables and booths. It is virtually empty at this time of the morning, and it is here that we first meet Renee, who in a day from now will officially become our daughter-in-law. She graciously embraces us and welcomes us home. Renee is more beautiful in person, and I'm struck by her vibrant energy. Jet is walking on the shiny white tiled floor in this blue converse high tops and a toy airplane in his hand. Renee calls him over to us and we softly say our hellos to this sweet blonde-haired, blue-eyed boy with the gentlest of spirit. Jet is more interested in exploring than talking with us. We watch him walk around chattering the whole time. After a few moments of talking about the journey and the day ahead with Reece and Renee, we sit down at a table, gathering our suitcases and backpacks in a pile. Renee holds Jet as he stands on the bench. He is shy, but not scared. Jet is talking away to Geoff, showing him the plane in his hand while his other hand holds on to his mumma.

Reece stands up and asks the three of us what we want to drink. *I'll have a flat white, thanks,* I answer.

We measure our visits home in years and coffee cups. Remembering and returning to our former selves melding into our new present.

UPRIGHT

JOY AND EXCITEMENT ARE FILLING YOU RIGHT NOW. THERE IS A VOYAGE IN YOUR FUTURE THAT IS TAKING YOU TO A PLACE YOU LOVE AND WHERE YOU FEEL LOVED.

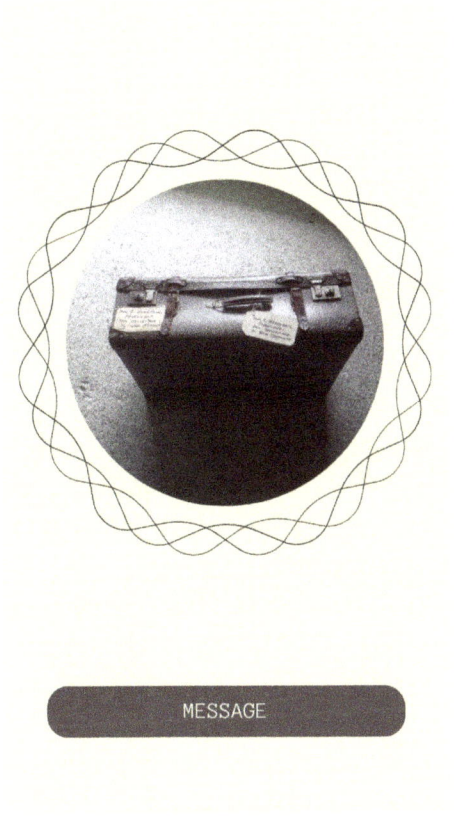

MESSAGE

REVERSED

SADNESS AND GRIEF ARE PRESENT AT THIS TIME. IT IS YOUR TIME TO MOURN A LOSS, BUT KNOW THIS IS A SEASON, THE PROCESS AND CYCLE OF LIFE. YOU ARE LOVED.

RE-JOURNEY

Twenty years after our wedding, Geoff and I sit on the beach at Browns Bay. This year our journey back to Aotearoa New Zealand is larger than us. We seek knowledge – ancestral, historical, personal. We return to the place of our honeymoon, Paihia, which rests less than 2 km from Waitangi – the grounds where the Treaty of Waitangi was signed by the Crown and Māori chiefs. I didn't understand the importance of the place when we were there twenty years ago. At the time, it felt like another visit to Independence Hall – a place where people, mentioned in history books, signed a document that created a nation.

The United States of America and Aotearoa New Zealand both start as colonies of the British Empire. The founding document of the nation of New Zealand is between the Crown and Māori. The founding document of the United States, the Declaration of Independence, is a document written by the settlers to express their grievances with the Crown, but there is no mention of Indigenous peoples.

This time I have a foundation of information and my memory of a young woman visiting the grounds of, what some might call, the birthplace of New Zealand. We map out our journey north through lands and landings of ancestors. This journey – a discovery, a re-remembering.

For now, in this moment, we listen to our grandchildren call to each other as they run into the waves. Curling hands of water reaching towards us as we look out beyond the beach to Rangitoto majestically rising in the Hauraki Gulf. I wonder what this place means to us. Do we see it differently because we no longer live here? Yet, family, past and present, continue to call us back, reminding us our path continues in Aotearoa.

MARKING MILES IN KILOMETERS

Technicolor, scrollable Google maps; ancient, dusty AA maps Geoff's dad gave me twenty years ago; black and white printouts taped together on the floor; miniature maps glued into my travel journal; spiral bound Kiwimaps driver's atlas with gloss pages and wrinkled topographic landscapes. I see the land as if I am a bird flying over it – dipping down into the valley, coasting on the sea breeze, soaring over mountains.

Places I never visited when I lived in Aotearoa New Zealand. When I lived there, my navigation points were footpaths, buses, taxis around Auckland. I was navigating a place where I lived and worked, with only rare moments to see anything beyond the city. I've seen more of Aotearoa since we moved away and our trips home are vacations.

I gather maps – finger tracing over land pausing briefly at the name of our destinations before swirling the tip of my finger up to the end of the North Island, Cape Reinga. Twenty years rest in our bodies, our marriage, since our last journey North. This year we will go further – all the way to the Cape. The place I've heard about, read about, but never witnessed. When I map out our trip, marking the days in the calendar, calculating the hours.

Geoff says, *We can easily go to Cape Reinga when we go to Paihia.*

I look again at the maps. Counted time on my fingers, *Are you sure?*

Of course, he answers. *We are Americans now – six hours of driving is nothing to us. Hell, we drove all the way from Quakertown, Pennsylvania to Bellingham, Washington. That is more driving than a Kiwi will experience in their lifetime. We drove fourteen-hour days on that trip.*

It is funny to hear him say we can handle hours in the car. In Pennsylvania – a visit, before we move back –we drive from my parents' house to Montgomery Mall in North Wales. Snowy fields following us for the seventeen-mile drive. Halfway there, Geoff asks if we needed to pack a lunch. We all pause our conversation and look at him confused.

No, we answer collectively, trying to figure out why someone would ask about packing a lunch when we just had quiche, ham, fruit and homemade bread for brunch.

Delayed reaction, we realize he is commenting on the amount of time we've been in the car. It would become the running joke when we move back to Pennsylvania – if it is more than a ten-minute drive, we warn Geoff that he might want to pack a lunch before we pile into the car.

When I finish our travel calendar for our trip in December, I share it with our family in Aotearoa New Zealand. The first comment we hear is – *You are going to Cape Reinga? That's a lot of driving.*

We smile.

We will pack a lunch, I answer.

CYCLE OF RETURN

We often travel to Waiuku and Karioitahi Beach on the back of Roxy, our motorcycle. Black sand sparkles and creates abstract tattoos around our ankles. Grey mist makes the grassy hills a mirage. Clouds float over our footprints. The thin layer of water reflects the sky back up at us.

The old two-story pub with wrapping verandas – The Kentish Hotel is my marker for Waiuku. It announces the town where Geoff used to live when he worked at the steel mill.

Near the corner is a claustrophobic antique store where I buy pieces of pottery. The owner's wife came over to see me one day to thank me for buying her pottery experiments. On a whim, she put her pottery out in the store, and seeing they sold, put out more, only to learn one person was buying them. Those pieces of pottery still peek out in places around our home. Does Geoff, like me, think of Waiuku each time he stands at the sink and picks up the vegetable brush from its pottery base?

Twenty years later, I wonder if the visits were a returning to a time and place where Geoff was happy before. Before me. Before his divorce. We drove by his old house once. Once. White, wooden with a fence. Was it too hard to see again? I didn't ask him at the time. Maybe I should have. But what did I know of loss and love then? I was new to marriage. New to life, really. My naivety just starting to loosen from my skin, but the shedding had not yet started.

It doesn't matter to me why we return to Waiuku, because each time we return, we return as us. We meet Gary one day at his place before going to his mum's for tea and biscuits. I marvel at her tea set. Geoff notices and buys me a silver tea strainer with drip bowl the next day. We start to create new memories to transpose over the old. Maybe that is his plan all along.

So, when Geoff says, *Let's go to Waiuku*, I happily oblige. On the bike, we drive south away from the chaos of the city. After a trip to the pub for a beer for Geoff and gin and tonic for me, we discuss the day as our salty fingers reach in for more peanuts; we wander to the little shop with the pottery. I gather my gold coins to see what I can afford. A trinket to hold my memory. Then to the beach. Our ritual: pub, shop, beach. Our feet sink into the sand – leaving a mark that the sea erases.

UPRIGHT

IT WILL ALL BE REVEALED. TAKE TIME TO SEE SOURCE AND MOVE INTO MEDITATION. ALL YOU NEED TO SUCCEED IS AT YOUR FINGERTIPS.

HIDDEN RITUAL

REVERSED
YOU'RE MISSING SOMETIHNG. IT IS IMPORTANT THAT YOU PAUSE AND LOOK AROUND YOU. RETURN TO YOURSELF.

FISH AND CHIPS

Sitting with our backs facing the water, the sun tickles our bare necks. We are no longer held in the grip of Bellingham, Washington's winter. We reach our hands into the layers of paper encasing our dinner – fish and chips. The grandkids eat more tomato sauce than chips. We didn't know or we would have bought another can. (They grow up so fast and we only see them in spans of years). Salt leaves a familiar mapping on our fingers, leading us to rub it between our thumbs. I slip out of my jandals. My feet, still sandy, swing over the blades of grass. We pass an L&P between us – a whim to buy a soda, but when in Aotearoa New Zealand, we prioritize taking in all the tastes of home. Geoff's journey through Aotearoa New Zealand turns into a quest for steak pies, milkshakes, fish & chips, filled rolls, krispies, hokey pokey, chocolate fish. For me, I relish in the flat whites, cheese scones, and pinot noir. I may not have the childhood memories with Kiwiana foods as he does, but there are things I long for, too.

TAKE ME TO THE CAPE

It is the everlasting hills of one's own deserted territory that welcome the wanderer home and it is the ceaseless crooning of the waves against a lone shore that perpetuates the sound of voices that are still

- TE RANGI HIROA

Geoff mentions we can drive to Cape Reinga/Te Rerenga Wairua on this trip home, which means I will finally see the northernmost tip of the North Island, and thus the top of Aotearoa New Zealand. I read enough books to understand the importance of the Cape to Māori. Te Rerenga Wairua is the place where souls depart for the spirit world. Spirits leave at the ancient, over 800 years old, pohutukawa tree that stands staunchly at the edge of the world.

I expect that we will see water for ages as we drive, but the road winds travelers inland. At moments when we look out to each side, we see slivers of bright blue waters. The land starts to drift behind us, and my breath catches in my lungs as if I've just been thrown into cold water. I try to dismiss the physical reaction in my body.

The road literally launches us to the sea. We lift up through the land to see the swirl of water below. We arrive at Te Rerenga Wairua.

As we reach the edge, tears glisten in my eyes. I don't know why the emotion of arrival and loss fills me. I shiver even as the sun beats down. The kind of shiver that starts at the bottom of my spine and rests at the base of my neck for a lingering moment to remind me I am a small speck in the greatness of the universe. A clairvoyant once told me that the shiver is a sign of communication from the other side. I remember that he also told me that the random ringing in my ear is a voice speaking to me, but I am not open to listening. A shiver – a sign or a whisper – stops me in the parking lot.

The beauty of the water below squeezes my chest. I squeal, running to the edge of the path. *Look at that*, I grab Geoff's hand and pull him towards me. Is he feeling what I am feeling? This place swirls with a magic I can't name.

I prattle on to Geoff as we walk the path towards the lighthouse.

I spend months before our trip to New Zealand writing about water and my relationship with Geoff. Water captivates me. My childhood is peppered with people complaining that I waste too much water, or I am part fish. It isn't until I move to the South Pacific that my love of water expands. I often have "moments" (I'm not sure what to really call them) when we are out on the water. As if my body finally feels that I am home.

In those moments I understand the need for gods and goddesses. I wrote a poem about it during a trip to Sydney called "She Beckons from Bondi:"

> I stand with wind whipping
> my hair on a boat
> bound for Bondi.

> Watching the water –
> cobalt waves dancing
> with emerald reflections.
> My first visit to the famous
> sun-kissed beach and I allow
> the experience to absorb
> into my pale skin.
> I am mesmerized –
> by the sea and the way it sings.
> I appreciate the ancient
> necessity for gods and goddesses –
> Surely something pure
> and holy must make the water
> dance so mysteriously.
> I close my eyes – the boat
> rocks matching the heartbeat
> of the sea goddess. I can see
> Her, and she knows me.

Because of my connection with water, I am not sure why I didn't take into account how I would react to seeing two seas meeting. Before we reach the point to witness their co-existence, we pause to read a sign on the side of the pathway. It says the Māori identify these waters as the place where the male sea, Te Moana Tapokopoko a Tawhaki, meets the female sea, Te Tai o Whitireia.

Are you kidding me? I say out loud to no one but myself. I spent months thinking about the link of water to my relationship with Geoff, our marriage, our understanding of place, our understanding of love . . . and here we are walking to the place to witness the male and female sea reaching for each other.

I kiss Geoff on the cheek as we walk down towards the lighthouse. He holds my hand. Together, we witness the joining of the two seas that we have spent our lives together watching from opposite shores. The Pacific Ocean on the east and the Tasman Sea on the west. This place. This marker of time. This union. Was us.

***

From the lookout, just beyond the lighthouse, waves crash into each other. In the distance, the current makes a U as if the Pacific is trying to swallow the Tasman. A mouth open-wide to welcome its lover. The impact of competing waves sends spray flying into the light blue sky. Geoff wanders around the lighthouse and reads the historical plaques while I plant myself at the cliff's edge. The water dances. I whisper to myself – *I'm here*. I pinch the skin between my thumb and forefinger.

Geoff returns to me. He leans against me, his hand on my back, and we watch the water. Giggling like children as the tall sprays reach for the clouds resting sweetly in the sky, I rest my head on his shoulder, *Thank you*.

We go to the water, Geoff and I. Our place for replenishment and rejuvenation. The edge of the sea, the goddess world. We witness the two seas in the same duality – beginning and end. Waves that plummet into each other; a fierce force echoes out to us – a clear sign of edges meeting, combining, and becoming something new.

Twenty years ago, Becky, this Pennsylvania girl, didn't realize the power of water or the land, but she traveled head-first, heart-first, into a new life. Destruction of self led to the creation of a transnational woman, Rebecca, with an obsession for the sea. A blended version of me now exists as I walk Aotearoa shores.

RESPLENDENT BREATH

*We must learn to speak the language women speak
when there is no one there to correct us*

- HÉLÈNE CIXOUS

I'm told to ground myself:
Root down to rise up.
Imprint my feet – enmesh
toes and heels into the stones,
sand, clay, humus.

But my feet are firmly rooted
in two nations spreading me wide
across the globe. I circle around
hemispheres. In and out of belonging,
in and out – legs
stretched, straddling. Feet planted
yet the pull heaves the ground,
roots lifting, like the earth filling its lungs.

My toes once kicked at the soil
where New Zealand was birthed
– Waitangi Treaty Grounds
Māori and Crown combining – on my
honeymoon. New land. New
life. Wife. Land becoming part
of me. Waitangi reminds me to return,
to honor, to feel here –
the arms of Norfolk pines raised and whorling
cumulus clouds, by the Treaty house.

Twenty years later – night before
I return to Waitangi – we sojourn in Swiss
Chalet – not the honeymoon suite this time,
but our bodies remember. Light sinks
and I whisper *Waitangi* leaving it to rest
on my tongue like melting sugar.

Just before the sun penetrates
the curtains in Paihia and our bodies
reach for each other, I leave the physical
world. Nana finds me in New
Zealand so far from her Pennsylvania
grave.

13 Dec 2016 – Last night I had a dream of my Nana.

Under a maple's lime green shade.
Air warm. A humid *subtropical* lull
much like Paihia in December.
Leaves overhead twist,
twinkle in sunshine. I remember
smelling roses. Purple violets
on oak picnic table. We,
my aunt was there too – younger

version of her, we commiserate
about our degrees. Taking classes
while working. Being more than
student. Nana raps her finger
on the table, *I wish I finished.
I wish I started earlier; when I was here.*
Where?
New Zealand.
Nana pulls me aside
tells me to find
balance. I open my mouth
to say, to assure – when
my husband's body presses
against mine. I return
to Paihia with a deep,
resplendent breath.

AWAKE

I woke up early. I was going to crawl back to bed to write, but I didn't want to wake Geoff. I thought about the café (Mud Bay – the only café in Urenui), but I didn't know if they were open on Sundays. So, I decided to walk to the beach to sit on the bench where Geoff and I sat last time we were here. Tiny spots of blue sky peaked out from the clouded sky. Low tide with a bite in the sea breeze. The birds trilled and tried their best to compete with the pounding surf.

The day before I explored Urenui with a Kaitiaki, Māori leader, and I received my DNA results – a glimpse at my own ancestors through a list of numbers and percentages on an electronic page.

    51% Germanic Europe
    30% England & Northwestern Europe
    12% Norway
    7% Scotland

***

The Māori Kaitiaki made a remark about the need to let the past wrongs go in order to move forward for a better blended society.

I contemplated the movement of time as I watched the ocean and land combine. Nation and land tried to stand firm as the surf pulled and pushed the land away and back onto itself. The white cliffs highlighted by the dawn sun; uncovered deposits of land, the past. Aotearoa's history opened wide by the sea. I sought the teal waves for answers and realized they already revealed it to me in the land left behind. Exposed, like me, firm in place but marked by layers of history, long forgotten, buried but awakened by the sea.

The land, here, has a story in the layers much like I have a story in the lines of land that rest beneath my ancestors' feet, and here I am on a foreign shore trying to add to the layers. To find where I fit in to two nations, two lands, two people.

Did we create a home? Did we have to destroy the old for the new? Where do we fit now? – we are unplaced, yet firmly placed in lands of our births.

Does this water shape me? I'd like to think so. It awakened in me a seafaring woman lost in the ages of cities, farms, and towns of Pennsylvania. Encrusted on top of the old – the water, the Pacific, the Tasman – reshaped me and exposed me to myself. Geoff helped me by taking me to the water – to the land of his birth, to an island in the South Pacific, to a new uncovered time. I travel between my two selves, two moments in time, my histories, two nations' histories – never knowing where I really belong.

FORMATION, DECEMBER 2016

Auckland skyline rests behind me. Sky Tower points the way home. The tide snakes dark water into the mudflats of Henderson Creek, creating a divide.

Land holds our stories, the dust, the dirt, our DNA. This land memory.

On the floor, feeling Auckland on my back. Jet, our six-year-old grandson, carries a large white cardboard box out of his room. His still-growing arms struggle under the weight. Curious to see what is hidden inside, I watch him slide the box the rest of the way into the lounge on the grey carpet.

Grammie, come look at this. Grammie, they call me, although I've never had children of my own. I remain Rebecca to my stepson, Reece.

Inside a kaleidoscope of gemstones, minerals, and rocks. He takes each treasure out and tells me its story. *This one I picked up when I was walking with Nana. And this one I got near the beach. Look, jasper. It has pretty brown lines.* When he notices he has more than one of the same kind, he hands a stone to me and says, *You can have this one.* I dutifully take the few he gives me and place them in a circle in front of my crossed legs.

Many in Jet's collection come from gem stores – polished amethyst, sliced agates, spires of crystal – but hidden amongst the purchased are the found. We might not share blood, but we are both collectors. My house is filled with jars, dishes, pottery chalices holding my secrets. Stones, shells, twigs, seeds from my travels.

I pick up an almost translucent stone with lines of blue, green veins. It looks like algae swaying in the tide, frozen in the briefest of moments. I ask about the type of stone and where he found it. He holds it in his hands, twisting it around just as I did, *I'm not sure, but you can have it.*

I don't want to take it, Jet. I just thought it was pretty.

I never found out the story of how this little stone found its way into Jet's collection, but it now has a story. Our story. Jet and me sitting in the lounge in Massey as we talk about collecting earth-made prizes.

In each piece we touch, we hear the story and add our moment to the littlest piece of mineral. Jet gives me a small piece of quartz crystal, the size of my pinky toe. He tells me that I need to squeeze real hard when I am sick or scared because it will make me feel better. He hefts a larger piece of quartz crystal and demonstrates for me, This is the one I hold on to when I'm sick. *Real tight, like this. See?*

What's this? I raise up a golden blob. It feels much lighter than a stone.

Oh, that's kauri gum. I have a big one here. He pulls out a piece the size of his fist.

Really? I have never held kauri gum before. I remember my husband telling me kauri gum is fossilized sap of the kauri tree. As the trees grow, they shed their bark and the gum adhering to the bark sloughs off. It starts to harden and through time it fossilizes.

Māori used kauri gum for generations – for chewing gum, for starting fires, for tattooing – before the Pākehā arrived. However, the kauri gum industry started around 1814 when settlers sent a shipment back to London. The kauri gum shipment supposedly ended up in the Thames, but that first shipment was the start of a Northland industry.

I roll the kauri gum in my palm. The gum, a resin created by the kauri to protect itself, now hardened, rests in my hand. What tree did it come from? Who dug it up? Why is it here in Jet's box of earthly minerals?

I hold the kauri gum for a few more minutes, rubbing my fingers on the glossy edges where it broke off from a larger piece before I place it gingerly back on the floor.

As we clean up the multitudes of orbs, I gather the few Jet selected for me and start to place them back in the box.

No, Grammie, those are yours. One collector to another, I accept the gifts. I gather them into a Ziploc bag and add a few more from our trip around Aotearoa New Zealand. Packing our bags to leave Auckland, Jet asks me if I still have my gems. I nod.

The stones Jet gave me sit next to my computer in a little green bowl that used to belong to my paternal grandmother, Grammy Helm. In the bowl amongst the shells and stones a golden nugget of kauri gum rests to remind me that land, even its piece, has memory. A story stored inside.

We collectors of treasures are also collectors of stories. Following the call to gather up a rock, a pebble, a shell. Each stone in my green bowl holds Jet's story and my memory inside of it. Such large work for something so small.

UPRIGHT

EVERYTHING IS IN PLACE. THE MESSAGES ARE CLEAR. TRUST YOUR HEART. LUCK AND FORTUNE ARE ABOUT TO TURN IN YOUR FAVOR.

MYSTERY

REVERSED

CONFUSION, AND UNCERTAINTY AWAIT YOU. YOU MAY BE FEELING UNLUCKY OR OUT OF FAVOR WITH THE UNIVERSE BUT KNOW THAT SOURCE WILL BRING CLARITY WHEN THE TIME IS RIGHT.

SLIPPING INTO HOME

I spend my summer trying to capture home in a narrative. I work through notes, photographs, and texts from my recent trip back to Aotearoa New Zealand. Wrestle with what it means when I say that word: home. Struggle with the concept of when an unknown place becomes a space where I feel at peace, safe, comfortable.

In November, I fly to Honolulu for the Pacific Ancient and Modern Language Association (PAMLA) conference. A trip I try to talk myself out of – too much money, bad timing, too many work demands – but something tells me I must do it. I prepare my conference presentation paper and book my flight.

A week before I leave my friend tells me I need to go to the Bishop Museum for my research. I balk at the idea because the conference is the reason for the expense and time.

However, I value her opinion and take her advice.

After two days of panels and paper presentations, I wake up on Saturday morning and open the sliding glass door to my hotel room. Humid air tickles my lungs and soaks my skin. Sounds of the city wash over me – the constant hum of traffic, the hiss of bus air brakes, the chatter of voices rises up the side of the building. Shouts from the construction site mix with the clashing of steel and the rat-a-tat of an impact wrench. The smell of the city – a mixture of moist green fumes, and the ocean's breath.

For the briefest of moments, I forget I am in a hotel in Honolulu and think I am sitting in our apartment on Queen Street in the heart of Auckland.

I don't know what to make of the ability to slip into a space of home even when not there – is that just a sensory memory?

One day, getting out of my car in Souderton, Pennsylvania, on a cool summer morning, just before the sun starts to heat the ground, something in the air smells like chocolate, making me think of my Pop-pop. Seeing his smiling face and the fluorescent lights glinting off his glasses each morning in the kitchen at summer camp. Picking up the olive-green Rubbermaid pitcher of hot chocolate at the "hot" window in the dining hall. *Good Morning, Pop-pop.* The chocolate smell in the parking lot on my way to work makes me smile at the memory.

Am I merely nostalgic for home? Can a sensory memory show intimacy? Do I have an intimate knowledge of Auckland? And if so, does that mean it is home within me?

***

The humid cityscape wave washing over me in Honolulu doesn't launch me into a sensory memory, but slips – yes, slips me back in time. Slipping into a parallel life. I am not sitting in Honolulu, but Auckland on our rimu slat bed, reading. It takes me looking up at my surroundings to realize I am in a foreign place. My mind clicks through seconds to return to the present moment in the Ala Moana hotel.

Home lives inside my body – my senses respond to it – it is the same sensation that jolts my body when I emerge from the Auckland airport. My physical body aligns with the spiritual, telling me that I am home, that I belong.

UNCANNY

6 June 2021

Sunday mornings are my moments to enjoy the luxury of reading in bed while the sunshine slowly starts to fill the room. On this spring morning, the birds were joyfully going about their daily rituals and making my cat jump from window to window, chattering back at them. Next to my bed was a stack of books that recently arrived from Aotearoa New Zealand. Picking up Charlotte Grimshaw's *The Mirror Book* that I was reading last night, I flipped to the bookmarked page and settled back into the stack of pillows.

I moved away from New Zealand in 1999, a couple of months before the world entered Y2K/2000. However, I stayed connected to the literature of Aotearoa. First, as gifts from my stepson. Later, shopping online became more accessible, and trips back home to Auckland always meant explaining to the customs agent that, yes, all I bought and brought back to the States were books. This spring, I was so excited to see more Aotearoa New Zealand memoirs in the market, and I immediately pre-ordered the memoirs by Patricia Grace, Charlotte Grimshaw, and Alison Jones.

Myla, my cat, settled down from the early bird frenzy. She sat across my legs, looking out the ranch slider to the deck off our bedroom. In the memoir, Grimshaw has just left an abusive relationship and is trying to find a new place to live. One of the reasons I love reading books from Aotearoa New Zealand is that I get to return to places I know. A story shared in some way. I looked up online the area she was living with her boyfriend in Auckland because it sounded like a place near where our friend Ed used to live. Ed was the best man at our wedding and a close friend to Geoff when we lived in Auckland. The area looked right, but I couldn't remember the exact building number for Ed's place.

Grimshaw's friend from law school offers her a room in his flat. She describes the building where his flat is empty and scheduled for demolition. Grimshaw states:

> We rode up eight floors and got out on the landing, after which we walked the final flight of stairs to the flat, a single-storey concrete structure, its ranch sliders opening onto a large roof terrace, with a view over the buildings of Queen Street.

I shifted in the bed, disturbing the cat, who let out an annoyed meow. Sitting up entirely, as if that would help me concentrate more, I reread the section. The "scheduled for demolition" is what first made me breeze over the text. A building that no longer existed on Queen Street. However, the description of the apartment – the elevator to the landing and the last flight of stairs to the flat, the ranch sliders to the terrace overlooking Queen Street – was all eerily familiar. Earlier, Grimshaw states, "It was an apartment built on the flat roof of a nine-storey office block, the CML Building, in Queen Street." An uncanny feeling washed over me on the third read of the paragraph.

Uncanny. A word often associated with Freud as a moment

that brings to light the familiar. Freud states, "the uncanny is that class of the frightening which leads back to what is known of old and long familiar." At this moment, the words on the page seemed distant and somewhat removed from reality. My brain understood that this was a memoir I was reading and therefore rooted in memory, the reality resting there. However, the mere physical pages of story created a distance as if the words were more fictional than fact. According to Freud: "This is that an uncanny effect is often and easily produced when the distinction between imagination and reality is effaced, as when something that we have hitherto regarded as imaginary appears before us in reality." I knew where Grimshaw was standing, "glancing into the bedroom, which was sunny and spacious, the windows open onto the roof area." I knew because I once stood there, too.

To confirm my place in that flat, I looked up CML Building, Queen Street, and found an article from 2011 when there was a fire in the building. The headline "Fire at Krukziener building closes Auckland's Queen Street," and images confirmed it was our apartment building. 163 Queen Street. The article also called it the CML building.

I was still confused. I thought she said the building was scheduled for demolition. When was this? Later in the chapter, Grimshaw mentions that she was living in the flat around the First Gulf War, which would place her there in 1991. I remember that time well. I was a senior in high school, and we had a school assembly when the war started. I moved to Aotearoa New Zealand in 1996. When I first moved there, Geoff mentioned that Auckland was in the process of converting office space to apartments to encourage a residential lifestyle in the center city.

After feeding Myla, I went into my office to start to research the building. Wardlow Friesen in his article "The Demographic Transformation of Inner City Auckland" states:

> *Towards the end of the twentieth century and into the twenty first century, a related but distinctive transformation has taken place in the CBD, with the rapid construction of commercial and residential buildings and a residential population growth rate of 1000 percent over a fifteen year period.*

No wonder the sounds of shouts from the construction site mixed with the clashing of steel and the rat-a-tat of an impact wrench remind me of Auckland. I looked up our first apartment on Lorne Street; Regency Apartments built in 1995. I moved to Auckland in the middle of an apartment boom. Friesen states: "Since the early 1990s, the number of residential and serviced apartments in the CBD has steadily increased, and by the year 2000 there were about 6,000 units." Grimshaw lived on Queen Street in the early days. According to Friesen, "By 1991, the usually resident population of the CBD was less than 2,000 mostly housed in a handful of surviving apartment blocks."

I still needed to figure out how it went from a condemned building to our home. We moved into the apartment complex in 1997. I loved that it had an old New York City feel to it. Our first apartment in the CML building, a one-bedroom, was on the 4th floor and looked out to the center of the building, an echoing abyss. Later, we moved into a two-bedroom across the hall with windows opening out onto Queen Street. This is the apartment we were living in when Auckland went dark. The now infamous 1998 Auckland Power Crisis. We, and everyone living in the CBD, were without power for almost six weeks between February and March when three major cables supplying power to the city failed in succession. Since our business was also in the CBD, one of the internet cafes, our livelihood and home both suffered in the blackout. Friesen mentions how we were part of the creation of the new life in Auckland, "Many other commercial enterprises, ranging from karaoke bars to two-dollar shops to internet cafes have also found niche markets in Auckland's CBD in recent years, catering to the new diversified inner city population." Later in 1998, the penthouse, as Grimshaw's old apartment was now called, opened up, and we jumped on the chance to live with a terrace over Queen Street.

After a few hours of internet searches, I finally found out that the CML Building, 163 Queen Street, was purchased in 1993. This would have been when the once slated for demolition office block – that Grimshaw recalls in her memoir: "On the way back down, Sean showed me some of the empty floors. The furniture and partitions had been cleared; shafts of light through dirty windows lit up cobwebs and dust"– was re-imaged and refurbished to apartments.

Geoff playing guitar in front of the ranch sliders Grimshaw mentions in The Mirror Book.

I figured out the timeline, which satisfied some of my questions. But now that I starting to think about the apartment, I was curious to look at some photos. This was prior to digital photography, so I had to wade through a sea of prints. I was sure I had general photos of the apartment. There was one in particular I was looking for – a picture of the dining room with the American and New Zealand flag on the windows. I never found the photo. The closest I found was a photo of Geoff and my stepson Reece. I believe these photos were taken around the time we were leaving Auckland.

There was a strangeness in reading someone else's account of a place you have lived. Not just the country, the city, the same street, the same apartment complex... but the exact same apartment. It was uncanny. A mirror stage through the eyes and experience of another, but familiar enough that the words transported me back to the sounds, smells, textures of the home we left behind.

I once was here.

- BEARDSALL & GRIMSHAW

Looking out over Queen Street from our 4th floor apartment in the CML Building waiting for the parade to start.

Addendum:

September 2022 – Aotearoa New Zealand for Geoff's mum's funeral.

In the process of cleaning out her house and reminiscing with each item of ephemera found tucked away in drawers, suitcases, and books, we found the photos of our apartment in Auckland, which intertwined my memories with Grimshaw's.

SECTION III

"But it's no use now," thought poor Alice, "to pretend to be two people! Why, there's hardly enough of me left to make one respectable person!"

**- LEWIS CARROLL,
ALICE'S ADVENTURES IN WONDERLAND (1865)**

WE ARRIVE AT THE WATER'S EDGE

The water guides us even today. We board planes instead of boats. We follow the red arc, the plane's trajectory, on the screen planted in the seat in front of us. We skim over the electronic ocean while the real one lies restless in the darkness below us until we reach the ground again.

But before us, before we meet, before we become a union, before we cry for a home left in the Pacific, before we learn how to enmesh our two cultures, our ancestors arrive via the waves of the Atlantic, Pacific, and Tasman Sea.

We trace Geoff's lines reaching out from Leeds, Nottingham, Belfast, Portaferry. We research ports, ships, births, deaths all their moments of departure and arrival. We gather papers, maps, and dates. The data points to Port Albert, Auckland, and Wellington. Before we arrive, they arrive, and it is our journey to watch where the branches intersect and graft onto each other to form the "we" who wearily walks off the plane. Our arms wrap around those we love; our eyes see the ponga, pōhutukawa, tī kouka – our lush green waking world; our noses take in jasmine, lemons, mud flats, and wet tarseal. We return as the water returns – our personalities continue to mix, alter with age, always desperately reaching for the shore.

UPRIGHT

IT IS TIME TO RIDE THE WAVES TO NEW HEIGHTS. WHAT YOU WANT IS ROLLING IN LIKE WAVES. ALLOW THE BLESSINGS TO WASH OVER YOU.

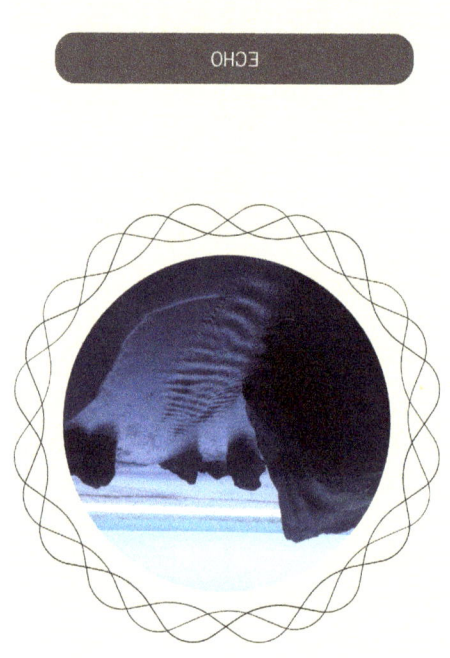

REVERSED

WATCH FOR RIPTIDES THAT CAN MOVE YOU AWAY FROM YOUR GOALS. THEY MAY SEEM LIKE THE RIGHT PATH, BUT THEY WILL SHIFT YOU OFF COURSE.

TRACING LINES

We sink our teeth into crumbs of Geoff's history, navigating the fading trails through time. The Beardsalls were the last to arrive on the shores in the South Pacific, so tracing their moment of immigration is easiest. We know they left Nottingham, already married, sailing to Australia on the S.S. Orient on 14 Nov. 1925. Internet searches for marriage certificates and ship arrival and departure records confirm our understanding. Then from Sydney on the S.S. Marama, the Beardsalls arrive in Wellington on 2 Feb. 1926. Dad makes his arrival fifty-four days later in Palmerston North. The first of the Beardsalls born in Aotearoa.

The Masons remain a mystery in their own way. We find them in shadows of others. Glimpses of what might be truth. We know that Henry left Portaferry, Ireland, via Belfast around the age of twenty, seeking his fortune in Australia. We learn that he supplies horses to the New Zealand government during the Waikato War. What we don't know is if he was already living in New Zealand at the time or if he was supplying the horses from Australia. Geoff remembers hearing about Henry's skills as a horseman.

We continue to circle around arrival. Who, of his lineage, was first to settle in Aotearoa?

I push Geoff to know. We hear no stories, no myths, no traditions. Our family knowledge is locked away in the memories of closed-lipped people. Instead, we turn to research. Geoff, recovering from a motorcycle accident, spends days lost in broken lines. Our office floor a pathway of papers creating intricate trails, where the Myrtle walks with dainty paws and meows.

Removing the cat, Geoff proudly points and pronounces the line, the link to who we assume arrives first – Bucktons.

This band of Geoff's family, members of the Albertland Settlers, a group of around eight hundred nonconformists who decide to take the offer from the Auckland Provincial Government of forty acres of land to every male, an additional forty for his wife, and twenty for his children paying passage to the colony. They arrive in New Zealand as passengers from the Matilda Wattenbach in 1862.

HELLO, MY NAME IS REBECCA, AND I'M A SETTLER

Three years after leaving Aotearoa New Zealand, I finally took steps to finish my undergraduate degree in English. A couple of years into the program, I took a creative writing course and started trying to write myself back to Aotearoa New Zealand. I spent days writing poems about rural Aotearoa New Zealand and the city streets of Auckland. Workshops of my pieces turned into me trying to explain to a group of Americans Kiwi slang. The novel nature of new words had my peers clamoring for more, but it wasn't the words I was trying to return to; instead, I needed to connect back with the land, the place, the people. And it seemed the only way for me to find a starting point was to remain in the fields of Taumarunui where I met Geoff's parents and where I experienced a version of Aotearoa New Zealand outside of the buzz of the city.

    I would continue to use my creative writing classes to reach into my memory and linger within moments in the Pacific. However, the last year of my undergraduate courses would take me on a journey I didn't know was possible. Each English major needed to take a seminar with a deep dive into literary criticism. The problem was I hadn't followed the standard timeline of the program because I was a nontraditional student, meaning I was older, working full-time while taking classes. I wouldn't be able to graduate after my senior year without this course. The department chair granted me, and a fellow student in the same situation, a theory seminar as an independent study. We would take the most critical course of our English academic career as an independent study, which would later come back to haunt me in graduate school.

The basics of Literary Theory were introduced in each of my previous English classes. I tended to lean towards Psychoanalytic, New Criticism, and Feminist theory in my papers. Our independent study meant reading a text, *Critical Theory Today* by Lois Tyson, and responding to what we learned on each of the approaches unpacked on the pages. The last chapter was on Postcolonial criticism. I had never heard of this critical theory and how it related to texts. The first section I underlined in the chapter, Lois Tyson states: "postcolonial criticism defines formerly colonized peoples as any population that has been subjected to the political domination of another population [. . .] for example, the literature of Australian aboriginal peoples." My marginalia reads *OZ and NZ*.

As a result of reading this section, I posted a rather unacademic response, but I felt I finally found what I was looking for – a flashing arrow pointing me in the direction I was desperately trying to figure out as I finished my degree. My post starts:

> *I haven't totally finished chapter eleven, but I'm just too excited for words, and I have to express my joy. Why am I so happy about postcolonial criticism theory? Well, this is exactly the type of critical theory I have been looking for, but I didn't know it existed.*

I used the examples from the chapter and discussed the work *Bulabasha* by Witi Ihimaera, a book I received that Christmas from my stepson Reece. It is a bit embarrassing reading through my post now, with what I know of settler-colonialism and Aotearoa. Still, at the time, I naively marched on about a topic I was only starting to understand. However, the last chapter in Lois Tyson's *Critical Theory Today* would give me the focus and drive to go to graduate school.

***

Walking on the historic, mountain-side campus where I would attend as a graduate student, I found the building that would be my home for the next two years. The quaint stone building was originally a student center in 1908. It served many purposes on campus through the years, and now it is known as the English Department building. Named after one of the University's presidents, I should have recognized the deeper implications of Drown's name on that humid, summer Sunday afternoon as I posed for a photo on the large terrace.

I was the first person in my family to go to university. I withdrew from Slippery Rock University when I moved to Aotearoa New Zealand. I decided to finish my bachelor's degree at the age of thirty. I worked full-time all through my undergraduate degree and was able to graduate summa cum laude. Yet, I was woefully unprepared for graduate school. I thought I would easily be able to maintain my 50 hours a week job and take a full load of classes, mainly in the evenings. I barely made it through the first semester without having a breakdown.

My days consisted of arriving at work at 5 a.m. and leaving working at 4:30 p.m. to drive to campus, over an hour away, three days a week. I'd go to class and arrive back at home after 10 p.m., where I would start reading for the next round of classes. The theory class my first semester was a mixture of first-year graduate students and Ph.D. students. I felt like I could only manage the mandatory readings, but I felt more behind in each class as all the other students shared additional books, articles, and research on the topic at hand. I started staying up until around 2 a.m., then getting a couple of hours of sleep before starting the cycle all over again.

Two weeks before the end of that first semester, Geoff found me sitting in the corner of my office, rocking back and forth. Crying. *I can't do this. I can't do this*, I repeatedly whispered. I went to work the next day and asked if I could reduce my hours to 40 per week. I thought about it; a 40-hour workweek seemed like a reasonable request for someone taking three graduate classes a semester. Those ten extra hours provided a bit of extra breathing room in my studies, but still weren't sufficient. My first year of graduate school finished, and I still felt like I was drowning.

I quit my job and found a part-time (32 hours a week) job closer to campus and my house. I finally felt like I could be part of the English graduate community and dive into my studies. It was time to start working on my thesis. I wanted to explore postcolonial theory in the South Pacific – this was the whole reason I went to graduate school. I longed to have the tools to work with and study South Pacific literature. So I talked to the leading professor of world literature and postcolonial theory in our English department.

Walking down the tiny corridor to find his office door tucked in the corner, I felt a sense of nervous excitement. I had already started requesting books and finding articles on the South Pacific. Sitting down in his office crammed with books and papers, I pulled out my notebook with scribbles of thoughts and ideas for the direction of my graduate thesis. I had taken his postcolonial lit class my first year and used some of the theories from that class to make my case. A thoughtful man, he nodded his head and listened intently. Once I paused and looked up at him with a sense of anticipation, he told me that my thoughts on this topic were interesting but that he couldn't help me. He said it was outside of his field. Crestfallen, I stopped listening. Wasn't this why I was here? To push. To delve deeply into a subject. I left his office without a thesis advisor.

My coursework improved as I had more time to devote to it. I started to love the class discussions again. I ended up working with another world literature professor on my thesis, but my heart wasn't in it. It was an exercise, not a passion. I started to shine that last year, but it wasn't enough to get me into the Ph.D. program. And I'm so thankful. I didn't realize it at the time, but the universe had other plans for me, for us. Geoff and I had purchased a house right near campus, with the contingency clause that our house in Quakertown sold; however, this was right at the crash and housing crisis in 2008. We were unable to sell our house and lost the newly built home near campus. Three years later, we sold our house in Pennsylvania and moved to Washington State – something we would have never done if I had been accepted into that Ph.D. program. And our move to Washington would prove to be life-changing.

My first graduate degree taught me many things about life and not much about literature. I wasn't any more prepared to wrestle with postcolonial theory than I was when I finished my undergrad. It taught me that you need time, space, and support to get the most out of a graduate degree to study, learn, and grow. Without time, it becomes a checklist. A to-do to work your way through without any enthusiasm.

I started a job in communications and marketing at Western Washington University. In new employee orientation, I learned about all the benefits offered to staff of the university, and one of those benefits was a tuition waiver. I immediately set my eyes on the Creative Writing MFA program and applied as the ink was still drying on my permanent employment acceptance letter.

At the age of 41, surrounded by a cohort of people in their early and late twenties, I was asked what I hoped to get out of graduate school. My answer – I want to enjoy the process this time around. I was a part-time student – only taking one class per quarter, three classes a year.

I found myself, once again, starting my second graduate degree, in a literary theory class. Unlike last time, I could easily keep up with the reading, and I had the foundation from the program to build on. I enjoyed the lively discussions as we sat in a large circle debating how Saussure's theory of signs would stop at the image; where Barthes' theory requires the audience to look deeper into culture ideology to understand the meaning of the sign/signification.

Our final research paper for the theory class was looming, and we needed to submit our prospectus. Following my motto of enjoying the process and graduate school this time around, I proposed, once again – six years later, to explore the literature of the Pacific with the lens of postcolonial theory.

Prospectus for the Research Paper:
The Postcolonial South Pacific:
A look at Rabbit Proof Fence

> Edward Said is considered the founder of Postcolonial theory, and his book Orientalism *is instrumental in helping the reader to navigate the world of the colonized and colonizer. However, as the term Orientalism implies, it is mainly the study of West and East. It is important to remember that the only way the "sun never set on the English Empire" was because England had territories in the South Pacific. Said mentions Captain James Cook, the British explorer who is the first European to reach Australia, New Zealand, and the Hawaiian Islands, in* Orientalism *when he discusses travel writings. However, the South Pacific is sometimes ignored in postcolonial work. I feel it is important that*

the South Pacific is part of the postcolonial conversation, and this is why I want to investigate this work for my final research paper.

For this research paper, I will look at Said's text on postcolonial theory in relation to Doris Pilkington's book Rabbit Proof Fence *(sometimes referred to as* Follow the Rabbit Proof Fence*). Pilkington writes about the true story of three Australian girls taken from their home as a result of the British Empire removing "halfcastes" from their aboriginal environments and assimilating them into white culture. At Moore River Native Settlement, the girls were forbidden to speak their native tongue and denied their aboriginal heritage.*

This paper will investigate how the British used domination and restructuring to gain authority over the Aborigines and how their misguided efforts to control and educate the children was destructive and continued to perpetuate the notion of otherness.

I waited for the dreaded response since it was clear from the conversation of postcolonial theory in class that no one saw it as relating to the Pacific. We all sat in a circle, watching the professor hand back our prospectus, holding on to hope that our ideas were worthy of a final paper. The response written on the top right of my paper: "This will be a fascinating project, and you're clear on what your research will add to the field. Nice work, Rebecca." I was in shock. I wanted to run up and hug my professor. I was finally going to be able to write about something I cared about. It turned out I was unable to write my final paper about *Rabbit Proof Fence*. Once again, god/universe had other plans.

From: *Rebecca Beardsall*
Date: *Wednesday, November 19, 2014 7:02 AM*
To: *Dawn Dietrich*
Subject: *Text*

Hi Dawn,

I may change my text from *Rabbit Proof Fence* to a New Zealand novel, *Once Were Warriors*. I'm having a difficult time getting a copy of *Rabbit Proof Fence* – a long story but the first book I got made me sick (allergies), and the second book arrived completely damaged in shipping, and I'm now awaiting my third copy of the book. I don't know if I should take it as a sign the book doesn't want to be read or that all the mishaps mean the book has great value. If it doesn't arrive today, I'm planning on switching and looking at the Māori/Pākeha relationships in *Once Were Warriors*.

Rebecca

Moldy used books, UPS damaged packages, and the pressure of a deadline turned me back to Aotearoa New Zealand.

I entered the MFA program with a plan to finish the book about my brother that I started as part of an anthology project with Colleen, my friend from graduate school in Pennsylvania. We edited two collections, and the essay I wrote for the one book was about Dwayne, who died in a farming accident at the age of 25. However, the second quarter of my MFA program didn't have any nonfiction writing seminars, so I decided to take one of the literature courses to fulfill the necessary requirements. ENG575 – Studies in Women's Literature. The course was set to start on January 6; however, Geoff and I would still be in New Zealand. We were heading home for Geoff's brother's wedding and wouldn't return to Washington until January 15. I'd miss the first three classes. I reached out to the professor to confirm that this would be okay. She approved the late start and sent the syllabus so I would be up to date on the reading when I arrived home.

Flipping through the pages of the syllabus, I stopped on Week 4. Eyes wide, I read something I never expected to see on a literature course syllabus. My experience at the school in Pennsylvania washed away in an instant when I saw the words Māori and the Pacific:

> Tuesday, January 27:
> "Introduction: Māori and the Pacific," "Māori People in Pacific Places," "The Realm of Tapa," "Māori-Pasifika Collaborations," "The Realm of Koura," "Conclusion: E Kore Au e Ngaro," and "Epilogue: A Time and a Place," from Alice Te Punga Somerville's *Once Were Pacific: Māori Connections to Oceania.*
>
> Thursday, January 29
> – "Part II: Reflecting" from Epeli Hau'ofa's *We are the Ocean: Selected Works*
> – "What Remains to Be Seen: Reclaiming the Visual Roots of Pacific Literature," by Teresia Teaiwa
> – "Navigating Our Own 'Sea of Islands': Remapping a Theoretical Space for Hawaiian Women and Indigenous Feminism," by Lisa Kahaleole Hall

I held up the stapled pages, shaking them towards the sky – not in rage, but pure excitement. I was in a graduate-level literature course, and we were going to read works from the South Pacific. Finally.

Studies in Women's Literature would give me a vocabulary and critical theories to begin a journey I wanted to be on six years ago. I learned that I had it all wrong. Aotearoa New Zealand couldn't be viewed through a postcolonial lens because the colonists never left; therefore, it could not be post-/after. Instead, it was settler-colonialism that I needed to study, and not only in Aotearoa New Zealand, but also in the country of my birth, America. I am/was a settler. I also learned about transnationalism and what it means to call more than one country home. Above all, the course introduced me to Epeli Hau'ofa, a Tongan and Fijian anthropologist and writer, whose writings helped me understand and articulate a non-western, non-linear understanding of time. And to Alice Te Punga Somerville and the term decolonization, "The project of decolonization in which all Indigenous people are engaged demands that grappling with, not the erasure of, colonization; it is about re-remembering."

My journey into understanding setter-colonialism and my place in that story took me back to where it hit me emotionally – Waitangi.

VOICE FROM THE PAST

My cousin recorded my paternal grandfather, who we called Pop-pop, and his children called him Pop. Pop-pop's voice, heavy Pennsylvania-German accent, leaping out into the future to share his life story. And ultimately, my story.

This is an interview with my grandfather, Harold Helm, born January 5, 1910, in Pennsburg, Pennsylvania. (Recorded February 7, 1981):

Now, this is Harold Helm speaking, and I will tell you about my grandfather, Albert. He came over (to the United States of America) from Germany in the 1800s and settled in Philadelphia. And he worked down there as a cutter for Wanamaker's clothing store. Him and his brother, Henry. Then he moved up to the country in the back of Trumbauersville on the Canary Road on a farm he inherited from his brother. His brother was murdered. There was just the two brothers. And he inherited his farm. It was a big stone building, and the barn was on the other side of the road. And he had about 105 acres. And he had five [sic - six] children. Annie, Ida, (Edward, Carrie,) George, Charles. Charles is my father, and he married

Emma Reinhart. And they had two children, myself and my sister. She was born July 6, 1906. She preceded me in death in 1940 when her daughter was born. She was married to Ralph Slaughter.

(*What was her full name?*) Florence Elisabeth.

(*Where was Albert from in Germany?*) He was born in Saxony. And he met my grandmother Elisabeth Schoenewald coming over on the boat. And they settled in Philadelphia.

(*What about his father?*) His father's name was Henry, and Elisabeth Schoenewald's father was Alexander. And this is how my father got this long name. Charles Henry Alexander Schoenewald Helm. He was the last one, and they wanted to give him the whole schmear.

My mother was born in Milford Township. And her father's name was Thomas Reinhart, and her mother's name was Mary Anne Barndt. The grandmother is a descendant of Phillip Leister. Phillip Leister came over in 1750. And he settled down in Milford Township in the part that is now Ridge Valley.

(*Did Grammy Barndt tell you stories?*) Yes, she told me, this was the time around Ridge Valley where the grandfather had the tailor shop; they had a log cabin. And there were Indians around that time. The Unami tribe . . .

OCEANS IN US

August 1990

Side stroking beyond the breakers, watching the sea of people on the beach, I am alone, launching my body parallel to the land along the water. Flipping over, sun tickles my face, my arms swing and cycle around. Water sloshing in and out of my ears as my body twists with each arm stroke. My breathing, so loud, feels like an echo, as if it is raining down on me from the heavens. Lost in the rhythm. Beat of my arms. Swoosh of my body dispersing water. Arc of water droplets raining down onto my cheeks. I flip over again to check the shore, trying to stay within the flags the lifeguard twisted into the wet sand, avoiding the rip. My friends look like miniatures in the distance. I'm far away. Do they see me? Are they worried my body is lost out at sea? There is no one around me. My arms and legs swirl in circles, closing in on themselves as I tread water. I finally see the flag and notice I went too far. I'm dangerously close to the power of the ocean. It could quickly lick me up and pull me out. I flip on my back again and use the power of my legs, muscles tightening, propelling me away from danger and back in the direction of my friends.

I'm back to the section of the beach we have overtaken for the weekend. I side stroke slowly, resistant to leave the peace of the ocean. Just me and the water. I see my four friends running into the breakers. Laughing, they dive into the waves. They huddle and tread water, bobbing up over the rolling sea. I wait a beat. A moment. Mourning. I swim towards them.

My body type is made for water. I am an inverted triangle: broad shoulders, narrow hips. Most professional swimmers have wide shoulders, long arms, leading to long, muscular legs. I am not saying I have the toned body of an aquatic athlete, just that I have the body type. An echo of my brother. Tracey tells me that is how she finds him in the mass of people in the ocean. She looks for his broad shoulders emerging out of the sea.

***

We are a family who vacations at the shore. New Jersey – Ocean City, Seaside Heights, Sea Isle City. Buckets full of seawater and shells. A thick quilted furniture blanket smelling of sand and sawdust welcomes our wet bodies onto its sun-warmed surface. Dad sits under a green, orange, and white beach umbrella. Seagulls circling for a dropped potato chip.

A family favorite – Chincoteague, Virginia. When I remember the ocean of my childhood, Chincoteague is part of that world. There is the year of the dead shark. Beach bound body with sharp, terrifying teeth. That is the only year my little legs stay on land. A hot summer week of no water, fear kept me digging in the sand near the Chevy Blazer that bounces us onto the beach.

There is the year of a shell bar so long and wide that I refuse to walk on it. It feels like a million crabs reaching out, pinching my not-yet-summer-calloused feet. An early teenage girl who needs her dad to carry her beyond the shells so she can dive under the water like a seal.

If we are not at the beach, we are at the pool – public or private – our bodies plunge into the water.

I teach myself to swim the summer between Kindergarten and First Grade. We are at the neighbor's pool. My siblings are swimming back and forth as I hold on to the side of the pool. Tempting fate by moving beyond the safety of the shallow end. I watch my brother launch away from me and return. Away and return – all legs and arms. Inch by inch, I return to the shallow end, my fingers pocked by the cement. When my tiptoes touch the bottom, I dip down underwater. Opening my eyes. Pushing off the wall, like my brother, and kick like hell until I make it to the shallowest part of the pool and stand up. I did it. That was easy. I plunge back down and kick off again. Again and again, I kick. My body giggles. I feel like I have answered the hardest question in the world. All riddles solved. I pop up by the edge and announce to my mom, sipping iced tea at the umbrella-covered table, *I can swim.*

Her response in the vein of *That's nice, dear.* I remember the disappointment by her non-enthusiastic response.

I discover a new mode of transportation. I discover my body inside water.

Later that night at the community pool, I show Dad my new swimming ability. *Good job, Pussycat. Now try to reach the other side.* I launch off, and he walks beside me ready to help me if I run out of steam. Finally, someone who understands the magic.

I realize years later that Mom doesn't know how to swim, while Dad, as an eight-year-old, was thrown over from the Richlandtown bridge by his father and told to swim. I had the luxury of a swimming pool with concrete sides to hold on to and to dare myself to explore the world under the water. Dad had a choice to literally sink or swim in the rain-swollen Tohickon creek.

Every first grader in the Quakertown school district takes swimming lessons at the local YMCA. In lines, we march out to the mustard yellow buses with our tote bags of swimming suits and towels. We blow bubbles in the water at the side of the pool before we are told to kick, kick, kick. Our tiny arms cling to the side of the pool while our legs work frantically to move us nowhere. We take turns out in the deep end with an instructor. With stiff arms holding a foam kicking board, we are told to kick hard. My neck strains to keep my head above water. Gritting teeth and half-open eyes, I try to say to the instructor I already know how to swim. I know this kicking with a board is not swimming. She tells me I need to learn how to swim on top of the water. *But I need to use my arms.* The whole thing seems stupid. My body wants to be under the water where I can feel free and fluid. I'm sure the instructor loves having smart arse kids telling her how to do her job. I promptly forget her instruction and stick my head underwater and swim over to the side where all my friends continue to kick and blow bubbles. It would be a year before I learn to swim above water. My brother teaches me in the neighbor's pool, where a dip in the pool is his reward for mowing their lawn. And his sisters take advantage of this perk and swim in the pool while he mows in the hot and humid Pennsylvania summer.

***

Now every morning, when I get into my car, I get a whiff of the beach. Or, more accurately, a smell I associate with the beach. Shea butter, coconut, and some other tropical fruit like papaya, pineapples, mangos. Our sunscreen-soaked beach chairs hang on the garage wall next to the driver's side of my car. In the middle of winter, snow falling outside the garage, I smell sunscreen and seaside air, closing my eyes for a moment to return to the place I love. The water. My sunscreen smells like the tropics, but I wear it in the Pacific Northwest sitting by the Salish Sea. There are no waves to surf and no sandy beaches. Our chairs rest on water-smoothed rocks, but the spirit is the same. The water calls to me, and I need it to replenish my soul. I return to the water weekly.

***

The grey, green, sometimes brown, Atlantic of my childhood is not the same as the deep blue, sometimes turquoise, Pacific. My love and adoration for the Pacific starts when I move to Aotearoa. The Pacific is where I found myself.

And it is the warm Pacific that I want to return to for my fortieth birthday. A momentous year in need of a renewal and rebirth by the Pacific. And I want to be on a sandy beach with the turquoise sea. We go to Hawai'i. Geoff and I walk a beach in Maui, and I announce that I want to go in the water. It has been almost twenty years since I swam in the ocean. He holds my towel as I tackle the waves. Giddy with my time in the rolling waves, I head back to shore. I hear a wave start to break behind me and think I will ride it in as I used to in the Atlantic.

My body is pushed down to the sand. My legs swing in the curl of the wave, trying to flip me around. Knees dig into the sharp shell sand. I use all my swimming knowledge to pull myself up and out of this twirling. My legs kick, and my arms reach out. I dig my fingers into the sand, trying to get some sense of grounding. Finally, the wave moves on, and I pull myself up and walk out. Sand streams in rivers out of my bathing suit. My hair full of sand and shells is pushed all around my forehead. Fear fading, I start to laugh. Geoff hands me my towel, and I give it back to him. *I need to wash this sand out first*, I announce as I stagger towards the makeshift shower at the edge of the beach.

Later, Geoff shows me the photo he took of me just as the wave consumed me. *I wonder if that is what Dwayne experienced*, I say, and then begin to tell him the story I heard when Dwayne and Tracey returned home from their honeymoon in Hawai'i. Tracey tells it from her lens. One minute Dwayne was standing in the bright blue ocean, and the next minute he was gone. Later, his body tumbled onto the beach full of sand. Dwayne talks about how he was tossed around by the wave. He relates it to being in the washing machine. I remember his laughter and Tracey's concern followed by laughter, when they recount the moment in our living room in Quakertown.

I want to share my Hawai'i wave story with him. Compare notes and wave wounds. I can hear us laughing. Wiping tears from our eyes. Perhaps I would hold my side and he would slap the table, and I'd wave a hand in front of my face trying to breathe.

And he would finally say, *It is like the ocean just spit us out.*

In the pause, I look at him as it clicks in my mind, *I think that is exactly what it did.*

Like it rejected us for some reason?

Right, because we were tourists. There to take and consume.

So it is about respect.

Yeah, respect the people, the place, and, I grin and raise my eyebrows, *the ocean.*

UPRIGHT

THIS IS YOUR MOMENT. YOU ARE OPEN AND YOU'RE TAPPED INTO YOUR SENSES. SEE THE WORLD WITH WONDER AND AWE.

FREEDOM

REVERSED

IT IS TIME TO RECONNECT WITH YOURSELF AND YOUR BODY. EXPLORE ALL YOUR SENSES. GO FOR A WALK IN THE WOODS OR ON THE BEACH TO REMEMBER THE WORLD AROUND YOU.

REMAINDER REMINDERS

In Pennsylvania, I lived on Lenni-Lenape land. The Lenni-Lenape are often referred to as the Lenape, which means "common people," but the addition of Lenni reinforces meaning and translating to "people common people." However, most Americans, if they know them at all, know them as the Delaware.

The name given to the Lenape derives from Lord de la Warr, who was appointed governor of Jamestown, Virginia. One of the Lord de la Warr's followers, Captain Argall, named the bay on the Atlantic coast after his governor. The Lenape, at the time, lived on the shores of de la Warr bay and the banks of the river that emptied out into it; therefore, they became known as the Delaware Indians. And the only reminders most people see that this land belongs to another nation are the names of places and rivers: Unami, Perkasie, Manayunk, Tinicum, Conshohocken, Minsi, Perkiomen, Susquehanna.

UNFURLING FROND

Air bubbles in the glass make it look like water. The blue and green take on the spirit of algae and seagrass. The bubbles hint to a life hidden below as if it rests at the root, the source of swirling colors. And then at the center of the koru, the tightly bound swirl, is the clearest of glass where I can see my reflection as it distorts itself into the spiral. An opening, but also a closing.

This is the heart of the koru – the unfurled fern frond. A sign of birth, beginnings, awakening.

Ka hinga atu he tete-kura - ka hara-mai he tete-kura.
    As one fern frond dies, one is born to take its place.

A year or so after we moved away from Aotearoa New Zealand, our friends from the Auckland City Mission came to visit us in Pennsylvania. They brought with them bits and bobs of Kiwiana to remind us of home. One item was a glass koru – licks of blue diving into waves of green. The marriage of greens and blues reminds me of the home we left in the South Pacific. Green hillsides rolling towards the bright blue sea; the multiple colored waters: greens, blue, turquoise; the bluest of skies kissing the leaves of kauri, rimu, ponga, kātote.

According to Les R Tumoana Williams and Manuka Henare in their article "The Double Spiral and Ways of Knowing":

> *At lower levels, the spiral can symbolize the life of an individual as well as that of groups who are also part of the cycle of life, growth, decay, death and rebirth. There are also many references to the natural phenomena of life and growth, such as the unfolding of the fern frond, leading to the process of decay and returning to the soil with the emergence of new growth, in a continuous cycle.*

The symbol of that continuous cycle sits on the shelf, reminding me daily of my connection to Aotearoa New Zealand, and my own rebirth and death that transpired there.

Years earlier, we walk amongst the cyathea dealbta (ponga), ferns the size of trees; Geoff tells me about the silver fern. *The leaves are silver?* I ask in childlike wonderment: What is this strange land I moved to?

He turns over the frond and asks if I can see the silver. It is not the magical silver I was dreaming of in the wilderness, fern-frenzied pathways winding around the bush.

The fully exposed fronds don't catch my imagination as we lean on each other, hidden in the shadows of trees. Instead, I marvel at the unfurled frond as it looks like a large furry, clenched fist holding smaller clenched-fists. *What is that?* I ask, and I can't believe it when Geoff answers, *A fern*. It doesn't look like any fern I have seen, but upon further explanation, I learn that the frond was the birth of the fern. It will become the large palms that weave the sky above us.

As I walk the streets of Auckland, the unfurling fern frond, koru, appears in carving, clothing, jewelry left in shop windows. Bone, jade, glass, plastic. A spiral within a spiral – movement in and out of each other. Contained and exposed. United and alone.

A symbol of time – spiral within spiral disclosures to the world: time and history. Each spiral a marker of the old and new in one moment.

In me, around me, outside of me – one dies, one returns. An echo and a shout of self. Both together.

A - *GASP* - FEMINIST

I attended my first March for Life in 1989. I had never thought about abortion, and I didn't have an opinion about it at the time. I was regurgitating what I was told at church and what my friends were saying. I was excited to get a day off school and go to D.C. I wore my little rose patch on my acid-washed jeans jacket but carried no sign or banner. We listened to President George Bush praise us for our commitment to the life of unborn babies. He stated that he felt Roe vs. Wade should be overturned, and we cheered. There was never a conversation about women's rights, women's bodies. But then again, women's bodies were only to be discussed in whispers. It was the first protest walk I had ever been on, and I was following a crowd, not a conviction.

Coming from a fairly compassionate religious sect, there were only a few things I was taught to dislike. One being feminists – those anti-Christian women with their men-hating notions and their unholy ideas about women in leadership, sexuality, and abortion.

I didn't come to my feminist sense until I was an undergraduate student returning to college in my late-20s and married.

I went back to school after we moved back to Pennsylvania. Sitting in one of my theology classes, my professor asked for a show of hands of those who thought of themselves as feminists. Only one woman raised her hand. (It wasn't me.) She looked around at the rest of us and said: Come on! She questioned our commitment to equality. Oh, I believed in equal rights and women having a voice. Yet, there was something about the term feminist that still haunted me from my childhood; enough that I didn't know if I was allowed (yes, *allowed*) to raise my hand.

After class, I couldn't stop hearing my classmates outcry at the lack of women raising their hands. Why didn't I raise mine? Fear? Uncertainty? A term I was taught to abhor? I walked into the cold, late autumn air through the dark parking lot. I threw my bookbag on the back seat and I got in the driver's seat. I sat there for a beat before I pushed in the clutch and started my car. As it revved to life, I asked myself, *Am I a feminist?* I said the word out loud, a mere whisper: *feminist*. Pushing down on the gearshift to click into reverse, my little red Volkswagen whirred as I backed out of my parking spot. I said it again, *feminist*. I shook my head and pulled out on to the road.

I debated with myself as I maneuvered around the dark, rural Pennsylvania roads. I realized it was my past holding me back from embracing what I knew was true. I was a feminist. It was just a word. A word I was taught to believe was bad. I came to terms with my feminist self, allowing the term, the naming, to apply to me by the time I pulled the car into our driveway. Pulling up the handbrake, I nodded in agreement with my own thoughts, and started the road of my separation from how I was raised. Another rebirth.

10 Dec 2016

On our first full day home, we went to the Auckland War Memorial Museum – an informative museum that sits in the heart of the Domain (on the rim of Pukekawa volcano), the oldest park in Auckland. Christmas in the Park was happening that night, and as we walked up to the museum, we watched as the vendors and crews readied the field for the festivities.

When we lived in Auckland, we would visit the museum from time to time, but most of our visits to the Domain were just for walking around or going to Christmas in the Park. Three years ago was the first time we had set foot in the museum since we moved away in 2000. That visit was with the grandkids, and we spent most of the time exploring animals. The last time we spent any time in the Māori galleries was when my parents visited in 1997. Almost twenty years later, the Māori galleries were the only section I wanted to see.

The night before I read Te Rangi Hiroa's chapter from *The Coming of the Māori* on Mats, Baskets, and Plaiting. I entered a world of techniques and patterns well beyond my realm of understanding. I tried to pull in my past knowledge of weaving from the summer I spent at my aunt's learning to weave on her four-harness floor loom. I studied the diagrams Hiroa provided to feel the way the flax joined. I didn't think much more about the chapter until we walked into that section of the museum. I was able to see it from a totally different lens. It was no longer a matter of reading the small plaques placed under the mats, nor was it an occasion to just look at the "pretty" woven pieces. This time I studied them and followed the lines, techniques.

As I stood mesmerized by the putorino (flutes) with their spirals for shoulders and thighs, Geoff wandered over to another section of He Taonga Māori – Māori Court. Of course, he found a spot with chairs and a small sofa where a film was playing. Geoff spends a lot of his time watching YouTube videos. This is how he studies and learns. I use books, Geoff views videos, and together we create a well-informed couple. He sat down and watched while I walked the image-based timeline that was around the section – I noted the 1975-78 protests in my journal (same timeline as the protests happening in the USA by the Native Americans). I jotted down notes about Dame Whina Cooper – a powerhouse and a matriarch – she spent her whole life fighting for Māori land rights. At the age of 80, Cooper led the famous 1975 land march from Te Hāpua (far north) to Wellington.

Then I started to hear the voices from the short film clips – *Perspectives on the Treaty of Waitangi*. Words pulled me towards them. Michael Dreaver, a former chief Crown negotiator, talked about the impact the Treaty of Waitangi had with Auckland iwi and negotiations that have been going on in the settlement process. We listened to Morehu Wilson speak about the influence of the missionaries and their message of peace and how it resonated with the Māori and that this influenced the Treaty. The Māori saw the Treaty as a way to consolidate their peace and as a reaffirmation of their sovereignty. We heard about the burning down of the village because the Queen was coming from Sharon Hawke, Ngati Whatua, as she recalled her father's memory of hearing his nanny wailing and trembling as she watched her house burn. She talked about the five-hundred-day occupation and eviction in 1978 of Bastion Point and how they used the Treaty process as a way of finding justice. She said, *Communication is the key. We need to drive our future by telling the story of how we began and telling the story of where we want to go... need to share the dreaming.*

Geoff and I sat so still listening that the film would stop

because it didn't sense movement. Geoff stood up and walked around, which started the video again.

As is my habit, I spend almost as much time viewing the exhibits as browsing the bookstore. This visit, I picked up three books. *Making a New Land: Environmental Histories of New Zealand* by Eric Pawson and Tom Brooking, *Tangata Whenua: A History* by Atholl Andreson, Judith Binney, and Aroha Harris, *A History of New Zealand Women* by Barbara Brookes.

Geoff and I shared our visit to the museum over dinner with Reece, Renee, and Renee's dad, Keith. I told them that we listened to the informative video clips on what continues to develop between the Māori and the Crown. Renee asked what section of the museum, *We go there all the time. I haven't seen them.* I told her it was in the Māori Court, He Taonga Māori. She responded, *Oh, we don't go in there. The kids always rush to the natural history galleries.*

We finished our meal. Reece, Geoff, and Keith continued their conversation as I gathered some of the dishes, and Renee asked if anyone wanted more wine.

As I walked into the kitchen, I asked Renee, *Did you know that they returned the Auckland Mountains to the iwi?*

What? Renee shouted as she grabbed the bottle of Pinot Noir.

Yes, that is what they said on the film.

What film?

The one we were just talking about, I answered.

I need to see that section, she said as she poured the wine.

What mountain is yours? I asked Renee.

She answered. Then she looked to her dad to confirm, *Is that right?* Keith nodded and shifted his focus to the conversation Renee and I were having in the kitchen.

I told them about the books I purchased at the museum. I

ran down the stairs to the guestroom and brought the stack of books back for Keith to see.

As Keith held the book, *A History of New Zealand Women*, Renee said, *I wonder if Meri is in there?*

Who? I asked.

Meri, my great-great-grandmother.

Renee's great-great-grandmother was part of the suffragist movement in Aotearoa New Zealand. They looked in the book and found her on page 134 – Meri Te Tai Mangakāhia of Te Rarawa.

Keith talked about his relative who knew Whina Cooper, and I had to sit down. As Keith continued to flip through the book, he casually mentioned that he heard that Whina Cooper had a lot of mana – that people said they could sense it when she walked in the room. I was silenced. I had so much I wanted to say and ask, but I lost it all in the moment. Here I was searching for understanding, and right next to me, my daughter-in-law's father was talking to me about Whina Cooper as if she were a family friend, so I froze in awe. I felt like I didn't have the voice to share this story.

Renee continues to share moments of Meri with me. Recently, there was an exhibit at the same museum about the suffragist movement. She shared photos of the kids standing in front of Meri's parliamentary chest.

Renee went to the museum bookstore and purchased a tote bag with Meri's images to send to me. She also gave me a print one Christmas called *Deeds Not Words* – an art piece by Angie Dennis. One bird and two women take up prominent space in the art piece.

The bird, the petite and chubby pīwakawaka (fantail), is my favorite New Zealand bird. The first time I saw a little pīwakawaka showing off its beautiful tail was on a visit to my in-laws in Taumarunui. It was love at first sight. I was constantly on the lookout for this cheerful, chatty bird whenever I left the city center where Geoff and I lived. Only years later, I learned the role the pīwakawaka played in the story and death of Maui. There are many stories of Maui doing incredible feats to benefit humans. He fished Aotearoa New Zealand out of the sea. He captured the sun and beat it into submission to slow down so that humankind could have more time in a day. Maui's last quest was to conquer death and provide immortality to humans. The goddess of the night and death Hine-nui-te-pō ruled the underworld. In order to gain immortality, Maui needed to journey through the vagina of the goddess Hine-nui-te-pō and exit through her mouth. His bird friends warned him of the dangers of such a journey, to which Maui replied, "If you laugh, I will indeed be killed. But if I pass right through her body, I will live, and she will die."

As Maui wiggled into the vagina of Hine-nui-te-pō, the

pīwakawaka began to laugh, waking the goddess who crushed Maui with her vagina's obsidian teeth. This was the first vagina dentata story I ever heard. Yes, I realize the story means that death is still a part of life. Yet, I see the pīwakawaka as a feminist ally warning the goddess of the man trying to take her life, her power away from her. I always knew there was a reason I had an instant connection with the pīwakawaka.

The print also contains the likeness of two women on two teacups. The women are Kate Sheppard and Meri Mangakāhia, two suffragettes. Both were instrumental in Aotearoa New Zealand, becoming the first country in the world where women won the right to vote in 1893. The title of the print, "Deeds Not Words," comes from a famous saying of the UK suffragette Emmeline Pankhurst. Kate Sheppard, born in England, emigrated to Aotearoa New Zealand in 1868. She supported and promoted women's suffrage with petitions, meetings, and letter-writing campaigns. Sheppard was the editor of *The White Ribbon*, the first woman-operated newspaper in New Zealand. Meri Mangakāhia, born in the Hokianga district, was a member of the Te Rarawa iwi. She was of Ngāti Te Rēinga, Ngāti Manawa, and Te Kaitutae origin. She was the first woman known to have addressed the parliament on her motion that women participate in selecting members. In her speech, she not only stated that women should be allowed to vote, but that they should also be sitting members of the Māori parliament. Mangakāhia argued that Māori women were landowners in their own right who were entitled to have their say in decisions affecting them.

It is impossible for me to go throughout my day without being reminded of the strength of these women and the role they played in changing history. I purposefully decided to hang the picture in my living room, the central place of my home, to honor women and feminism. I was a late-blooming feminist, and my time in Aotearoa New Zealand was the start of it all for me. I would not be where I am today without my transnational identity spanning the United States of America and Aotearoa New Zealand, and without the strength and courage of the women in both nations to bring about change and stand up for the voices of women. Pīwakawaka, Kate Sheppard, and Meri Mangakāhia bear witness to my days and remind me that I am stronger than I think. They remind me to lift up and support other women and to be a voice allied with the silenced and marginalized. Feminist, that's me.

UPRIGHT

IT IS TIME TO FILL YOUR CUP WITH THE ELIXIR OF LIFE. PLAY IN THE MAGIC AND MYSTERY THAT SURROUNDS TIME. A SEED IS BEING PLANTED THAT WILL BRING YOU ALL THAT YOU DESIRE.

MYSTIC

REVERSED

DON'T WALLOW IN THE MYSTERIOUS. SEEK CLARITY, AND A WISE FRIEND WILL APPEAR TO GUIDE YOU ONTO THE NEXT PATH TOWARD SUCCESS.

THE LETTER BEE

There are books that stay with you for life. In July 2003, I took a twentieth-century literature class as part of my undergraduate program in English. In that class, we read Myla Goldberg's *Bee Season*. Eighteen years later – I am still thinking about the characters, their lives, their actions. I've kept a piece of this novel with me all these years. So much so, that when we adopted our second cat, when deciding on her name, I went to my library and ran my fingers along the spines until I stopped at Goldberg. *Bee Season*. It seemed a sign. Our new kitten's mother's name was Bumble Bee. Myla. I named our kitten.

This last weekend I was drawn to the book once again. A small voice – I'm not too fond of that term because it isn't small; it is grand and booming, but because it isn't a voice at all, we call it small – or something kept telling me to return to *Bee Season*. The push was insistent enough to put down the current book I was reading and pick up my well-read, supple, starting to yellow, pages of *Bee Season*. I removed all the post-it paper tags I had throughout the pages that once supported me in writing my seminar paper on the novel. On this read, I used the more enhanced plastic-like clear flags with colored tips. My preferred markers since you can still read the text underneath. I settled into the novel like revisiting old friends. However, the reading soon turned towards enlightenment. Pages morphed into mirrors. I started to understand why these characters had haunted me for 18 years. This family – The Naumanns – were a family of four individuals living in the same home but living totally separate lives. Eliza is an average student who we later find out has a natural talent for spelling – she sees the words. She longs for the affection of her parents, particularly her father. Her brother Aaron is smart, talented but searching for something bigger than himself. Saul, their father, is philosophical and easily gets lost in his reading. Miriam (oh, Miriam) is on a quest for perfection, and she is smart but distant; everything is in the world to be researched and analyzed. Each of them is on their own spiritual quest to fulfill their desires and to know themselves.

Watching the movement of this family where no one is aware of the other. Each person is living out a dynamic, complicated, vibrant life inside their head. I start to look back at Rebecca – Becky – Rebecca. I see a bit of myself in these characters. I arrived in the world self-sufficient. To the point that I used to rock myself to sleep when I was a baby. My mom tells the story of when they had dinner guests, and someone asked at the table, *What is that noise?*

Oh, that's just Becky rocking herself to sleep.

My crib had wheels that carved grooves into the pine floors with each side-to-side movement. A bed and body in motion to lull me to sleep. I would continue this monitoring and regulation of my sleep for the rest of my life. While most kids begged to stay up late at night, I usually walked into the living room and announced it was time for me to go to bed. Mom has always told stories of me playing alone in my room, and when she would later come to check in on me because it was a bit too quiet – she would find me tucked into bed, taking a nap, or sleeping on the floor amongst my toys.

I played alone. It may have seemed a sad and boring life

to the watching eye, but my mind was constantly moving, creating, and living in my imagination. I was the only person in the house of five to live in all three bedrooms at one point in time, and it was because my parents saw that I spent all my time in my room. They grew concerned when I moved out of my shared room with my sister to my brother's room when he moved out, his room being the smallest, coldest room in the house. That they offered me the largest bedroom with the large bay windows overlooking our street.

No wonder I saw myself in this fictional family of individuals who just happened to live in the same house. That echoes back to the way I grew up. It also explains why no one knew me and my feeling of not belonging. I lived my life internally more than externally. And it would be years... years... until I reconciled the person I was and the one everyone wanted me to be.

Twice in the book, Miriam starts to think her family understands her. Once she watches Eliza in the spelling bee, she sees herself in her concentration and peace that comes over her body when she knows the answer. However, when Miriam gives Eliza a gift, an essential piece in her life, and there is no instant recognition from her daughter, Miriam realizes that no, they are not the same. Later, Saul will bring Miriam a shoebox containing a ball, another critical object in Miriam's life, and there is hope in her heart that her husband finally knows her. But Saul has used, bounced the ball, and it is the end for Miriam – no connection. She realizes she is alone in the world.

Eliza will also make a stand for herself. She, like her mother, will face the world alone without needing the approval she once craved because she has surpassed her father. She has moved into a new plane of being. In this, Eliza mirrors her mother: "Looking into the bus window, Eliza sees Miriam reflected in her own face. 'Hello,' she whispers to the window.

When she smiles, her mother's reflection in the window smiles back."

When I had my natal chart read, I was told my childhood home/life was in Chiron, the great wound and place of pain/suffering. I didn't understand it. I said, *I had a great childhood. I wasn't particularly ill as a child.* As I talked it out, I realized that it may have been related to not belonging, feeling unknown. Basically, living my life in my family much like each member of the fictional Naumann family.

In the book, by the time Miriam is in college, she and her parents realize that "in their attempt to give the best of everything, they have never gotten to know (her)." My Chiron, my wound, being unknown but loved. Miriam instead turns her analysis back on herself, her childhood, her parents: "Her annual visit home is like a trip to her favorite reference library, her parents [sic] primary sources to be examined. Through them she confirms her roots, observing enough of herself in them to assuage her general sense of at-oddness with the world." I have never felt so seen in a line of a novel before. That voice that told me to re-read this novel, I believe, was pointing me to this passage. I have spent the last ten years on this journey of analyzing my life, where I came from, how I became Rebecca. I finally started living my inner life outwardly. But in order to do that, I needed to move away. To leave the social norms and confines of my familial life to branch out in a place as an unknown so I can be known. It all started in Aotearoa New Zealand, and came to its final realization in Bellingham, Washington.

SPIRAL

I have an obsession. Something that always sits in my mind waiting for a moment when I can dance with it again. An ever-willing partner in my analysis of myself and the world. Time becomes the sea that I continue to return to, watching the waves arrive and return into themselves.

Recently on my walk, I was listening to the podcast *On Being with Krista Tippett*. The session was in an interview with the 23rd Poet Laureate of the United States, Joy Harjo, and they titled it "The Whole of Time." Anything about time and I'm listening, reading, watching. So, as the interview started to move to a close, I was thrilled when Tippett pointedly asked Harjo about her perception of time. Tippett mentioned that she felt Harjo holds a sense of different types of time, including the concept of "the whole of time."

Epeli Hau'ofa's discussion of the circular nature of life in his book *We Are the Ocean* made me realize my way of looking at the world wasn't unusual; instead, it was just different from my culture's understanding of time. Instead of placing so much value on the future, Oceanic cultures emphasize the past. Often my insistent need to understand what came before was brushed off as nostalgia or romanticism. American culture and society looked forward – always forward – not back. When I tried to connect with the past, I heard *why care about the past when the excitement of the new was in the future?* When I read that Oceania cultures valued the past to understand the present, I shouted "yes" loud enough to startle the cat sleeping beside me. Here I found the theory, terminology, and foundation for an understanding of time that had existed inside of me. It wasn't Western linear time but instead circular time and later the spiral time that would bring me into a new understanding of myself and the world around me.

In the chapter "Pasts to Remember" Hau'ofa states, "That the past is ahead, in front of us, is a conception of time that helps us retain our memories and be aware of its presence." He stresses the need for people to investigate and understand their past so that they can not only situate themselves in the present but can move into the future. According to Hau'ofa, "What is ahead of us cannot be forgotten so readily or ignored, for it is in front of our minds' eyes, always reminding us of its presence. Since the past is alive in us, the dead are alive – we are our history." Not only is it history, but it is also memory. To remember people – the past, the stories, the myths – is a place to house the present and ultimately the future.

The past is always in front of us, and the Māori understanding of the spiral brings that into clarity. We are our past, our history. Here. Now.

History will always find you, and wrap you
In its thousand arms.

– JOY HARJO, "BREAK MY HEART"

PENNSYLVANIA PAST

I grew up in the shadows of Philadelphia, Pennsylvania. The heart of a nation always under my footsteps. Less than a block from my street stood the house that stored the Liberty Bell overnight on its journey to Allentown. As Philadelphia prepared for a British attack, the Continental Congress grew concerned that the British might melt down the bell for ammunition to use against the colonists, so in 1777, the Liberty Bell left Philadelphia. The bell secreted away and hidden for the duration of the Revolutionary War, but before it could reach its final hiding place it rested in Quakertown.

Legend has it that the Liberty Bell tolled on July 8, 1776, to summon the citizens for the first public reading of the Declaration of Independence. I used to climb the replica on Broad

Street in Quakertown. I touched the cold metal bell in Philadelphia and read "Proclaim Liberty Throughout All the Land unto All the Inhabitants thereof" as I traced my finger along its crack.

Countless class trips to historical sites in Philadelphia are part of my childhood memory.

Cheese and mustard sandwiches packed with frozen Cokes wrapped in aluminum foil so they would thaw and remain cold while we walked the pathways of our founding fathers. The wooden floors of Independence Hall where we smelled the dust residue from the late 1700s. Our class listened to some man dressed up in a white wig tell us the birth story of a nation. The history of the founding of the United States of America became a narrative I absorbed into my life like my skin absorbed the smells of Philadelphia: the baking dough of pretzels, the fumes of SEPTA buses, and the tang of cured meats. History present with every visit, it all required such little reflection.

I have a clear memory of trying to separate story from story in Gettysburg – another Pennsylvania town where I spent countless hours walking the fields marred by the Civil War – a different birthing story of the nation. My uncle went to the Lutheran Theological Seminary in Gettysburg, which meant we visited often. One day my parents, brother, sister, and I rode a double-decker tour bus visiting the sites and signs of the Civil War, where we witnessed cannonballs still stuck in the bricks of houses and businesses downtown. While riding the bus, we listened via large plastic headsets to the story of July 1-3, 1863, an important moment in the Civil War and a major turning point for the Union.

    I listened to stories about generals making decisions about Cemetery Ridge, Little Round Top, and Culp's Hill while hearing gunfire, cannon blasts, and horses neighing; it felt like I was listening to my books on record. I loved listening to stories. I had a large collection of books that had records or tapes with them; I diligently waited for the "turn the page" chimes before I moved the graphic story forward. The paper crinkled under my fingers. But instead of a book to look at, I had hills, long expansive fields, groves of maple trees, and bright white monuments while the narration animated the scenery.

As we continued to travel the battlefields, the August sun sank into my skin, the oversized headphones pushed my head into my shoulders, and I was lost in the story. I smelled the gun smoke, saw men hiding in the trees as the narrator told us about Pickett's Charge, a march across open fields. I didn't want to listen anymore: I knew bad things were going to happen. The thumping of my heart started to drown out the story. I pulled the headphones off and heard the whine of the bus engine. My mom looked down at me and smiled. I put the headphones back on, their weight pushing me down further on the hot plastic bus seat. Horses screamed; men screamed.

I pulled the headsets back off – the stillness frightened me. I tugged on my mom's shirt, her red cotton shirt with a collar, my favorite because it made her eyes sparkle. She pulled her headphones off, and I asked, *Is this real?*

What do you mean?

Is this a true story?

She smiled and nodded, *Yes, this is a true story.*

While I couldn't actually see Pickett's men walking that field, I felt them and their fear.

TOUCHING HISTORY

Jennie was the only civilian killed in Gettysburg. When Geoff and I went to visit the Civil War site a few years ago, I told him we had to go to the Jennie Wade house because they had a real-life funeral set up in the basement. The basement was filled with people dressed in period clothing, which included a few in Union uniforms.

My fingers ran along the edges of the stones, and the brick floor had a thin layer of tan clay dust that I slid my toes into. A colorful quilt was draped over the body of Jennie. A man with a beard stood closest to her (perhaps a doctor or minister) and held a brimmed hat in his hand. A woman in the burgundy dress put a hand to her nose. Or was it to cover her mouth? All these years, I assumed they were wax figures, like many of the historical "people" in Gettysburg.

But when Geoff and I walked into the basement of the Jennie Wade house, we found it empty except for a painting depicting the funeral on the stone wall.

I could say that I fictionalized that painting and made it real, but there was no lady in burgundy or doctor/minister in the picture. Instead, the painting showed a young boy sitting on a wooden chest, and Jennie's sister, dressed in white, holding her newborn baby with two Union soldiers behind her. Another man sat on a bench at Jennie's feet. It may have been child-like wonder or a muddled memory, but I know what I sensed that day when I was seven years old in the basement of the Jennie Wade house, and it mirrored the sensation I felt a year before while listening to the (reenacted) battle on a double-decker tour bus.

Moment of time locked in the place where it happened. Memory, individual or collective, held tight until it can be shared, absorbed. Jennie's funeral existed inside of me, a receptive seven-year-old girl.

UPRIGHT

IT IS LIKE SPRING! THE FLOWERS AND TREES ARE IN BLOOM, AND THE BIRDS ARE SINGING SWEET MELODIES. THIS IS A TIME OF REBIRTH. OPEN UP YOUR EYES, EARS, AND HEART FOR GIFTS ARE COMING YOUR WAY.

LISTEN

REVERSED

IT IS IMPORTANT THAT YOU PAUSE TO LISTEN TO WHAT IS GOING ON AROUND YOU. THERE IS A MESSAGE YOU MISSED. RETURN TO THE BEGINNING AND LISTEN AGAIN.

MEMORANDUM

To: ~~Becky Helm~~ Rebecca Beardsall
CC:
From: Rebecca Helm Beardsall
Date: 30 November 2016
Subject: RE: 30 November 1996

****

In light of your recent visit to Waitangi and the Treaty Grounds, I felt it necessary to address your behavior.

    First, thank you for visiting Waitangi while you were on honeymoon in Paihia. Your husband's national history should be important to you, and I hope you will be able to return the favor someday by sharing the historical places of your nation, the United States of America.

    I can appreciate your fascination with the gardens around the Busby House/Treaty House. The foliage was vibrant during your early summer visit. However, this leads me to my concerns. I feel you missed the point of the Treaty House. It wasn't the gardens that you should have been looking at, lovely as they are, but instead you should have paid attention to what was inside the house. (Did you see the replica of the Treaty? Did you see where the Treaty was written?) Yes, the peach rose was remarkable. I understand, but did you know the rose, often considered a common flower, was *introduced*, by early missionaries, to Aotearoa New Zealand in 1814 (emphasis mine).

The neglect on your behalf to recognize the settler colonialized situation in Aotearoa New Zealand is, quite frankly, abhorrent. Since you are a US citizen, I would have assumed you understood that struggle, but then again maybe you weren't taught the truth in school. I guess the idea of a treaty might be hard for you to understand because of how they were ignored in the land of your birth.

But that aside, you listened to your husband talk about the Treaty being written in Māori and English, and you just nodded your head, but didn't really hear him. You didn't take the time to ask about the translation – was it accurate? Who translated it? Heck, you didn't even ask what the Treaty was about or what it meant to Aotearoa New Zealand. Did you even know it was between the Crown and Māori?

You stood at the spot where the Treaty was signed, and instead of feeling the moment, you looked out at the blue sea and watched the boats drift. Yes, the Pacific is mesmerizing, but you stood at the spot of the birth of a nation, and you missed it.

The land you stood on altered a nation and its people, and all you could think about was a photo opportunity to send back to your parents in the US: their daughter on honeymoon in New Zealand. *New Zealand, can you believe I am living here, Mom and Dad!* I am not against sharing memories, but if you want to show off that you live in Aotearoa New Zealand, you should at least take the time to learn about its history.

The footsteps of Hobson landing on the beach in the Bay of

Islands altered the course of a nation. Did you even go to the place where he walked onto the shore? You use Māori words, but you are ignorant of their history. Did you look at the waka? Did you ask about it? We both know that you did not.

You walked the grounds of Waitangi without a thought about the people who call Aotearoa New Zealand home. And for that, I am truly heartbroken. To rectify this situation, I recommend that you study settler colonialism, learn about the history of Aotearoa New Zealand, and then return to Waitangi.

Kia ora.

TIME TRAVEL

I linger in the odd, mistrusted places of time – the spaces no one wants to talk about or recognize, let alone be seen lurking in its corners. I started visiting the secrets of time when I was little before the realities of the world removed them into fantastical musings. They are always with me and have been my whole life, but over time I've tried to justify them and ground them in the reality that we have collectively decided, albeit without much thought, to agree upon and establish as the norm.

In a moment of bravery, I wrote about my slippage through time. Instants when the world around me hazes over as if watching it through a veil, and it is just me, in vivid reality, watching something unfold that I should not have access to, and I feel the event in the core of my being. It is usually the sounds around me or lack of them, I should say, that alerts me to an access point. Often all sound stops. I exist, in an instant, in utter silence. Other times sound muffles or mutes – people's voices around me become like a hum.

Ironically, these moments I experienced were easier to explain when I was active in the church. People are willing to believe

God gave me a sign or spoke to me via another form. It also didn't freak me out when I could say, *Speak, your servant is listening* – like Samuel.

Even now, as I try to write about these moments in my life when I have felt time move like the sand shifting, I fail. People can stand on the shore and see with their eyes the waves rolling in, constantly, never-ending like time itself. However, it is not until they step into the water, at the very edges, that they can sense the opposite. There is an undertow moving away from what they see rolling towards them. There are two movements at once. This is how I often experience time. Rolling. Slipping. Unseen to many, but there are a few of us who dare, or who are chosen, to stand at the edge of time only to feel it shift beneath our feet.

TIME TO FACE IT

9 a.m.

The expansive glass Visitor Centre welcomed us. High ceilings created an openness inside – a refreshing breath. Neon pink day pass stickers announced that our visit included a guided tour, access to the museum and treaty grounds, and a cultural experience. Geoff and I furrowed our brows at each other – didn't we just walk around last time? Neither of us remembered a tour; maybe we had opted out. Was it even an option twenty years ago?

We were asked, *Are you from New Zealand?*

He is, I paused then I added, *I'm a permanent resident, but we don't have our passports with us.*

Okay, where are you from?

Auckland, Geoff answered. And Bellingham, I thought.

The tour didn't start until 10 a.m., which gave us time to explore the new museum.

THIS IS WAITANGI.

***

KO WAITANGI TĒNEI

THIS IS WAITANGI

Welcome to Waitangi, Te Pitowhenua, the birthplace of our nation, New Zealand.

Here we tell of the relationship between two peoples, Māori and British, who came together to found a nation, and of Waitangi's special place in that story.

The story continues to unfold. It is a story for everybody – for all who call Aotearoa New Zealand home, for all who visit.

Come and share in it.

Nau mai ki Waitangi, Te Pitowhenua, te wāhi i whānau mai ai tō tātou Niu Tīrenitanga.

Ki konei kōrerohia ai te whanaungatanga i waenganui i ngā iwi e rua, te Māori me Peretaina, i hui tahi ai ki te whakatuwhera i tētahi whakaaetanga whenua, me te motuhaketanga o Waitangi ki roto i taua kōrero.

He mea whakapuaki tonu taua kōrero. He kōrero mō te katoa – mō te katoa ka mea ko Aotearoa tō rātou kāinga, mō rātou katoa ka tae manuhiri mai.

Haere mai me tō whai wāhi ki roto i a ia.

Welcome sign on the walls of Te Kōngahu Museum of Waitangi

I stuffed my notebook in my messenger bag and quick-walked towards the sunlight that poured through the glass doors. I looked back longingly at the last half of the museum. The lighted displays beckoned. Geoff returned to the darkened treaty document room, *It's time.*

Everyone waited outside. A young man dressed in all black, wearing dark sunglasses, greeted us as we picked up headsets from a plastic tray he held out for us. I awkwardly attached the earpiece and fiddled with the sound until I could hear our docent's voice. *Kia Ora*, he started and launched into his story and history. A local Māori with ancestral connections to Waitangi. *Where are you from?* A few people answered Germany, England, the South Island.

Great, anyone else from New Zealand?

Geoff and I half-raised our hands while we looked at each other for confirmation.

At the beginning of the tour, we were presented with the basic history of Waitangi, and I realized, looking around at the others, that my first visit didn't provide me with this information. There was no museum with replicas, images, videos showing the reenactment of the treaty negotiations. These people were already ushered into a better understanding. I also realized that unlike the people – Kiwis and foreigners alike – that this might be the one and only tour where I was well-versed in the history steeped into the soil.

A fern-covered track led our group to the currently empty carving studio. The silent studio lost amongst the trees. Ushered out of the shadows of ferns and trees into the morning sun to the waka, Ngātokimatawhaorua, the world's largest ceremonial war canoe built for the 1940 centenary of the Treaty signing. The taurapa (sternpost) carved and painted black was our first point of introduction. The waka, an astounding size that holds 80 paddlers and room for 55 passengers, majestically pointed out towards the sea. The size of the Kauri trees that were used to create it must have been massive. It took five men over five hours to fell the kauri used for the center section of the waka. They used traditional methods in the construction, which meant they must have spent time in the bush as they prepared the tree. What did it feel like as they shaped the wood amongst the other trees, the kauri's fellow rootmates, and listened to the sounds of the birds, offspring of Tane? The final construction created a waka that weighed close to six tons.

It's launched every year on Waitangi Day.

The waka was renovated a year after my birth when Queen Elizabeth II visited Waitangi where she designated it Her Majesty's Ship, making it part of her Royal Navy.

As everyone listened to the history of the waka, I watched the water. The docent waved the group to move beyond the middle of Ngātokimatawhaorua to the end, closer to the water, so we could examine the intricate carvings. Next to one of the supports of the waka house, I struggled to keep myself grounded in the moment instead of drifting off towards the sea.

What happened next transpired fast and in a flurry of movement. At the end of the discussion of the awe-inspiring waka, the docent made note of Hobson's Beach as he led us away from the water: *It is called Hobson's Beach, because this is where Hobson came on shore, and he traveled up this trail to where the treaty was signed. Let's head up there now.* The group followed.

I froze. Here. Here. I looked out at the water as if I could see Hobson's ship out there. I read so much about what led up to the signing of the Treaty. Texts that provided me with the images of this scene in 1840. Claudia Orange's commentary on the treaty swirled around in my head:

By Thursday morning, 6 February, the chiefs had come to the decision that the treaty business should be concluded immediately so that they could return home. Williams was informed accordingly and by mid-morning between 300 and 400 Māori had gathered once more on Busby's lawn. Scattered in small groups, according to their tribes, they waited. On the Herald, however, there was no sign of movement. When Shortland, Cooper and Mathew came ashore towards noon to 'see what was going on', they were surprised to find the crowd waiting. On the ship they knew nothing about the meeting. A boat was quickly sent for Hobson who confirmed this fact; he had 'not the least notion' of a meeting being held . . . Events now moved towards the signing. The official party took their places in the marquee. There was none of the pomp and circumstance of the previous day's meeting. Hobson, taken by surprise, had come ashore in plain clothes except for his hat.

The moment returned me to my childhood experience in the Jennie Wade house and the battlefield in Gettysburg. It felt like I witnessed it in real life. In the present. I saw Hobson rushed onto the beach, heard the boat's bottom scrape the rocks, shells, and sand. I watched Hobson's feet touch the ground, caught unawares for one of the most important moments in Aotearoa New Zealand's history. He straightened his hat, standing up tall as he did so, and then he proceeded to walk up the pathway, now called Nias Track after the commander of the Herald, with long, purposeful strides. As I looked at the water and the bright sand, the vision vanished, and I heard the voices of the people around me as they started the trek up the hill. I wanted to shout, *You are missing the moment*, but realized I had missed it twenty years ago as well.

I waited for most of the people to walk ahead of us. Geoff, confused, watched and waited for me. In relative silence, we walked up the gravel path. Just as they walked here, our steps crunched the pebbles and shells further down into the earth.

This – the moment.

Here.

SHORT-e /e/ BECOMES /ɪ/

Geoff never knew me as Becky; he has called me Rebecca from the moment we met. I refused even to tell him that I was once Becky until we were months into our relationship and when I did inform him, I pronounced a strict command not to call me Becky. Firmly Rebecca in Aotearoa New Zealand, I worried, when we moved back to Pennsylvania, home of Becky, about the regression of my name and the person I was becoming silently slipping back to my old persona.

Welcomed back to my hometown as Becky, I struggled to push people to remember to call me Rebecca. In the end, it wasn't me that would bring about the shift for Pennsylvania family and friends to stop referring to me as Becky. What started the change – or should I say who – was not me but Geoff. More specifically, his New Zealand accent. People became enamored with the way he pronounced my name, and they started to mimic it.

Often referred to as a twang, in relation to the British English of the colonizers of Aotearoa New Zealand, it is often the way the vowels are pronounced that cause the most confusion. According to Elizabeth Gordon, an Emeritus Professor of Linguistics at the University of Canterbury, "In the past people complained that the New Zealand accent was due to laziness or bad influences. Today it is thought to be based on the accent of south-east England, where most migrants came from." The "kit" vowel is often the one most linguists bring up to discuss the difference between New Zealanders and Australians: "It is commonly claimed that New Zealanders say 'fush and chups' where Australians say 'feesh and cheeps.' However, Geoff's pronunciation of the short-e had many of my American friends and family intrigued and confused. I've heard it referred to as the "DRESS vowel." According to Elizabeth Gordon, in her article on New Zealand speech:

> The TRAP vowel is raised (pronounced with a high tongue position) in NZE, and outside New Zealand is often mistaken for the DRESS vowel. A New Zealander overseas, Pat, asked people to address him as Patrick instead because he disliked being asked why he was called 'pet'. The DRESS vowel is also raised in NZE and can be confused with KIT – which is why New Zealanders overseas are given pins when they ask for pens.
>
> A recent change is the further raising of the DRESS vowel into the area of the FLEECE vowel, so that 'best' can sound like 'beast,' and 'bed' like 'bead.'

Everyone was used to hearing my formal name as Ruh-Bek-A, and this new version of Ree-Beak-A, sometimes sounding like Ree-Bik-Ar, sounded exotic.

Americans trying to sound like New Zealanders when saying my name is how I finally transitioned from Becky to Rebecca in my hometown. A girl called Becky moved to New Zealand to become Rebecca.

UPRIGHT

BEAUTY SURROUNDS YOU. HONOR THE LOVELY LIFE YOU HAVE. YOU HAVE LISTENED TO THE STILL, SMALL VOICE AND ARE REACHING YOUR GOALS.

WHISPER

REVERSED

IT MAY SEEM LIKE ALL YOUR EFFORTS HAVE REACHED AN END, BUT THE OUTCOMES ARE STILL BUILDING IN THE SILENCE. NON-ACTION DOESN'T ALWAYS MEAN YOUR PROGRESS HAS STOPPED.

DO YOU HAVE YOUR CAMERA?

Early in my MFA, during a workshop on a poem about my honeymoon in Paihia, my peers ask about the treaty I refer to in the lines. As I answer, my voice cracks, and I start to cry. Tears that caught me unawares. Crying over a treaty. In a graduate school poetry workshop, I realize that I need to write into my emotions and my understanding (or lack of) around a place, a space, a land, a country. Aotearoa.

I travel to Aotearoa to mark my twentieth wedding anniversary and return to Paihia and Waitangi. I plan to write about my experience for my MFA thesis. Prior to leaving, I meet with my thesis chair to discuss my writing plans. I schedule the days out and paste maps in my journal – a mapping of my return to where it all started: my marriage; Aotearoa New Zealand, the nation formed with the signing of the Treaty of Waitangi. In my meeting, I share with her my reading list. Her finger runs down the list; she pauses, *Oh, you should take and read* The Coming of the Māori *while you are there.*

I nod and dutifully jot down the note in my journal. I intend to fulfill her request until I return home and see the size of the book. I bought a hardcover cover edition of Te Rangi Hiroa's (Sir Peter Buck) 1949 book at a used bookstore in Bellingham, Washington. The printed price of the hardcover book in 1970 was $4.75, and that is what I paid for it in 2012. The book weighs two pounds, eight ounces. (Yes, I put it on a scale.) I decide it is too heavy. Instead, I place the book with its faded paper cover on my bedside table, planning on reading it in the next few days before our flight.

At night before bed, I pick up the book, flexing my arm to assess its weight. Still uncertain about what I am advised to do and my decision. I read Rt. Hon. P Fraser's forward. The first sentence: *"The Coming of the Māori* embodies the life-long research, study, considered opinions and conclusion of the greatest authority not only upon the Māori people and their history, traditions, customs, culture, social organization, and economic life but on the whole of Polynesia and the Polynesians."

Whoa. That feels like a serious throwdown. I see why my chair told me I needed to read it. I feel guilty that I had this book for four years just sitting on my bookshelf – a random used bookstore purchase. I often wander into Henderson's bookstore in my new-to-me town of Bellingham because on my first visit, I notice they have a New Zealand section. Almost every time I am guaranteed to find a gem. Clearly, I did in 2012, but I didn't know it.

I continue reading. Sinking into the pillows, I read the first paragraph of the first chapter, "The Discovery of New Zealand." I close the book. A little dust drifts across the beam of light from my bedside lamp. I am not supposed to read it here on a winter's night in Bellingham. I know instinctively that this book is meant to be read on the soil of Aotearoa.

An extra two pounds, eight ounces, Te Rangi Hiroa's words, travel with me back to Aotearoa New Zealand.

The next time the black marks on the page are exposed to the light is on the beach at Browns Bay. Grains of sand settle into the pages. I read through the three settlement periods while the joyful screams of our grandchildren ring through the air as they splash deeper into the water. Already my understanding of this land I long for expands. The history oozes out of the pages and links me more firmly to the sand I dig my toes into as I watch the waves roll towards me.

I carry the book with me for the rest of our trip up North. Port Albert. Kaipara Flats. Ruakaka. Cape Regina. Paihia. Waitangi. Waimate North. Tomarata.

Each time, as if by unseen guiding hands, I read a section, and then I experience the very elements in real life. I wander through pages about the intricate flax weaving skills only to study them a few hours later in the Auckland Museum. I learn about Māori warfare techniques and leaders, which I later discuss with a docent at the Te Waimate Mission.

Our journey up North ends back in Auckland, but our trip continues to visit my husband's brother who lives in Urenui, Taranaki region.

I pause at the pile of books. I finished reading *The Coming of the Māori* the night before our early morning flight to New Plymouth. The thought of not lugging the six-hundred-page hardcover book seems like an excellent idea, but not carrying the book, my constant companion on this expedition, feels weird. I can't decide what book, from the few I recently bought at the Auckland Museum, to take with me. I leave *The Coming of the Māori* on the guestroom bedside table at my stepson's house in Massey. I look at the book one last time, nod my head to acknowledge our linked journey, turn off the lights, and shut the door.

We all meet on the patio for breakfast. Breakfast consists of Oyster Bay sparkling cuvée brut, grilled croissants, eggs, bacon, avocado, and salad. As we gather around the table, Rodney, Clive and Steph's neighbor, calls out from his deck a few houses down the hill. We say hello and talk about going to the marae with him later in the day.

Prior to the trip, we have Geoff's brother Clive ask Rodney if he would be willing to take us to his marae. I have never been to one, nor has Geoff. A marae is a communal space, usually fenced in, which is sacred to the iwi to which it belongs.

Before heading down to Rodney's house, I think about taking my camera, but I don't want to be rude or misstep. I'm not totally sure of the protocol. I guess I can snap a few pictures with my phone if Rodney is okay with it. Putting on sunscreen, I ask Geoff if I should take my notebook. I have been recording events and details of each day. He says, *No, it doesn't seem right.*

I can write about it when we return. I agree.

We chat with Rodney and his wife Karen for a while on their deck, the summer sun warming our skin. Steph invites them over for dinner. Rodney asks if I have my camera. I hold up my phone, slightly regretting my decision to leave my camera behind. I don't know at that moment; I am about to go on a journey around Urenui with a Kaitiaki, a Māori leader. Rodney grabs his tokotoko (carved walking stick) before we get in the car. Geoff insists I sit in the front. *Are we all ready for our tiki tour?* asks Rodney.

All smiles, joy, and anticipation bubbling up from my core, I answer, *Yes.* After we pull out of the drive, Geoff asks Rodney about his role in the iwi, and that is when we find out he's a Kaitiaki.

We drive to the White Cliffs/Parininihi. Rodney notes that they are named after Dover, England. Standing outside

Rodney's car, we look over the landscape; he tells us how the invaders came in through this waterway. Also, it is this spot where the local iwi used to gather their food. We travel on to the site where missionaries used to live. They were eventually killed because of their association with the Pākehā (white colonizers). As Pākehā continued to devastate the land and its people, the local iwi retaliated and killed the missionary family. We pull up to the sign explaining the narrative of the missionaries.

I wish I had brought my camera.
Rodney laughs. *That's why I asked.*
I had no idea the journey we were going on.

At a lookout over the Mimitangiatua River where Te Kerkerewai Hapu lived, Rodney points to the hill on the other side and mentions that is where his brother rests as Kaitiaki of awa. I ask if this is his river, knowing that each iwi has their own river and mountain in their whakapapa (genealogy). I know Mt. Taranaki is the mountain in the whakapapa, but I don't know about the river.

Yes, Rodney answers, albeit a bit startled. Then he starts to recite the beginning of his whakapapa. It is beautiful. Standing here looking at the river and the space where the mountain should be, imagining what it must be like when Taranaki is visible. Today the glorious stratovolcano is hidden in a sea of clouds. Rodney is kind enough to help translate it for me. I frantically try to type it into my phone. I should have brought my notebook, I think to myself. Mimi River (Mimitangiatua) is also referred to in the Ngāti Mutunga pepeha as Mai Wai o Mihirau (Mimi River) ki Te Wai o Kuranui (Urenui), koia tera ko te whakararunga taniwha. The lifeline to the people. Water moving, pulsing through the fertile land. Water and land commingling amongst the people. A connection between the sea and the mountain.

Rodney takes us through his ancestral land. Driving through the green paddocks, I want to ask about Sir Peter Buck/Te

Rangi Hiroa, but every time I work up the nerve to ask Rodney, Geoff asks another question. Geoff is filled with questions on this trip. I can see and hear him experiencing this new part of the country he calls home. I want to find out if they, Hiroa and Rodney, are from the same iwi, Ngāti Mutunga. I know from reading *The Coming of the Māori* that Hiroa is originally from the New Plymouth area. As we start towards Rodney's family land, he discusses the swamps and how the Māori buried most of their sacred items, like carvings in the swamps. The swamps became a promising way to preserve the treasures and carvings. It is all starting to make sense. When we were at the Auckland Museum so many of the items on display stated that they were found in swamps. At the time of reading the plaques, I didn't know that it was on purpose that the items were hidden in the swamps. And that burying them was a way to preserve them from the elements and to hide them from the missionaries who were driven to destroy what they perceived as idolatry and unchristian. The sorrows of religion and colonization taking over a culture evident in the plain woodwork throughout the area. A constant reminder of what is lost, but also of how far Aotearoa has come since those days of conflict.

We drive through an old Māori village, Te Hawera, which means the breath of fire, by the house where Rodney grew up, before we go to the Okoki Pa Historic Reserve. Rodney points out the different pa areas up in the hills and hidden amongst the trees. I have never seen one in person that I know of, only what I witness in miniature at the museums. Rodney tells us how they create the pa. They level off the land and create trenches. Driving along the lush Aotearoa land, Rodney weaves stories of life on a pa. Warfare mingling with a lifestyle in the intricate construction of a pa. Safety for the collective planned into the design.

Okoki Pa Historic Reserve entrance is a sea of waving grass, but there is a mown track winding up the hill. Okoki Pa is an old and strategic, notorious fortification built by the earliest Māori settlers, Ngāti Mutunga, in the area. The Battle of Te Motu-Nui took place in the land between Okoki pa and the ocean. Records show that members of Ngāti Mutunga lived in the pa until the 1930s. We follow this mown river of grass until we can no longer continue up the steep hill. Ahead of us, on the hill, is a red and white sculpture that looks like the prow of a waka (canoe). I step out of the car into tall waves of grass and immediately my nose starts to run and my eyes water. My allergies dormant by the ocean air awaken in the fields of green. Sneezing, I listen to Rodney mention that this is the gravesite of an important Māori, the first Māori physician and a member of parliament. I marvel at the list of growing accomplishments as we walk up the grass-covered stairs.

Rodney walks ahead of us and chants a Karakia (incantation and prayer) before us. He turns back to face us. *I am just offering up a blessing to the ancestors and telling them we come in peace and not harm.* I feel his words wash over me, creating a space for our journey to take place. Keeping my eyes on the hidden steps, I watch my feet disappear in the tall grass.

Near the top of the steps, Rodney pauses and tenderly lifts a leaf filled with bug holes. Clearly, something is enjoying chomping on this bush (or is it a tree?). The shiny leaves dance in the light. *This is kawakawa, which you can boil up as a tonic and drink it.*

What does it taste like? Geoff asks from behind me. I almost forget he is there. I am so lost in the moment of walking up to this sacred space.

Tastes like peppermint. You can also use it to treat burns, cuts, rashes.

Rodney turns the elongated heart shape leaf over. It looks so small in his hands. The deep veins shooting from the center stand out even amongst the holes. *You can use the matte side as an antiseptic,* flipping the leaf again, *the smooth side can be used as a dressing.*

At the top of the hill, on Rodney's instructions, Geoff and I climb onto the concrete canoe. We can see the whole valley and shoreline from this waka monument. It makes sense why they created a pa here. The majestic world displayed before them, plus the strategic benefit of a vantage point that allows them to see everything coming towards them from land and sea. Geoff and I turn our backs on the land and sea to face Rodney to have our picture taken, the prow of the waka creating a strong line by our side. He mentions that he often brings people to this place as part of his tiki tour of the area. Geoff asks about the other graves, and we step down from the waka to view the older-looking gravestones. Some are boxed in with fencing. Geoff asks, *Why?* Rodney says the whole section is a gravesite – just unmarked. We are walking over the dead. Geoff grows concerned. Rodney continues, *Where we parked is also gravesites of fallen warriors.* The Battle of Te Motu-Nui (1822) when invaders from the Waikato were defeated by the Ngāti Mutunga. The whole place is an urupa (burial ground). History hidden but not forgotten. I can feel the place buzzing with the lives of so many.

We walk down the stairs into the trenches and underneath the concrete waka. There is an inscription at eye-height. A gasp stops me as my lungs try to recover from the surprise. I read it again to confirm the shock ringing through me, *This is where Sir Peter Buck is buried!*

Rodney, once again seems taken back from my reaction, *Yes*, he says as he points at the Māori name Te Rangi Hiroa. My hands and arms start flailing in front of me as my body tries to contain my excitement and I look for the words to explain to Rodney what this moment means to me. *I've been reading his book on this trip. I just finished it last night. The book has been guiding me this whole time.* Hiroa my constant companion as I travel the shores of Aotearoa. *And now... Now this. I left it on the bedside table,* I continue hoping to express the immediacy of my Hiroa experience to Rodney, *and now I'm here at his grave.*

I can't believe it. I am kind of glad I never got up the nerve to ask about Hiroa while we were driving around because to find out this way is so perfect. It mirrors how Aotearoa is slowly exposing itself to me. I am finding new things and seeing it all with a different understanding from the twenty-three-year-old who moved here twenty years ago. I care about the history that runs deep through the land. I can join the conversation thanks to Hiroa and many other New Zealand authors, friends, and family. Hiroa's detailed and focused narratives help broaden a once limited lens – a glimpse into the past and the people. So, one more time he, hidden in the tall grass of the pa, reveals himself to me. My guide. A nod to the journey I am on and where I continue to go. The spiral continues whether we realize it or not. We are connected. We loop in and out of lives and moments. On this journey Hiroa and I dance the sacred interstellar waltz of serendipity.

We do eventually go to the marae. It is the second to last stop on our way home. We have our photo taken at the old wharenui (meeting house). A building dug down into the earth with a small door wooden, white door. Two small square windows, like eyes, one on each side of the door. The whole front is trimmed in white with a koruru at the point of the gable. Maihi, signifying arms, reaches down on each side of us as we sit on the little bench to the left of the door. The sign above the door reads MAHI-TAMARIKI, which translates to "do children." This could mean making children or child labor. It is unclear. Rodney laughs, informing us that Urenui translates to large penis, so it is likely the wharenui "do children" links to sex.

I am not sure if it is because of my reaction, uncontrolled excitement, at the grave of Te Rangi Hiroa or maybe it is the questions both Geoff and I are asking, but as we sip beers on Rodney's deck with the warm summer sun across our backs Rodney decides to bring out his korowai/kākahu (cloak). Specifically, a kahu huruhuru, a kākahu adorned with feathers. It is beautiful, with layers of peacock feathers trailing down the back. I can't believe I am seeing one in person. I believe my eyes must be twice the size as normal as I soak in the cloak. Rodney talks about the occasions when he wears it. Holding it tenderly in his hands, he mentions that it goes on coffins, but it must be turned upside down so that the energy, aroha, is not taken away from it. Geoff asks for clarification as I nod my head, fully aware of the power that rests and circulates between those feathers. Rodney shares about the energy that the cloak draws and the importance of the power held there. He looks at me and says, *Do you want to put it on?*

Are you serious? I place my hand over my heart. Protection? Or just checking it is still beating, I am not sure.

Yes, he laughs a glorious ringing laugh that floods the space with warmth.

Oh, my goodness. I'd love to. I can't believe the honor I've just been granted. Rodney helps place it on my shoulders, and I feel a warmth expand over me. Geoff is instructed to take photos. There is a lot of laughter and delight coming from Geoff and Rodney while I stand there in awe. I'm afraid to move for fear of disturbing the moment – the magic. I am frozen holding the cords of the cloak close to my solar plexus. Lingering in shallow breaths. I turn in intervals when Rodney tells me to do so.

Taking off the cloak, my fearful ridged body relaxes yet I mourn the loss of the... power. Yes, power. That is the word bouncing around my brain. I am back in the ordinary, but in the briefest of moments, I touch a magic few will know.

Marrying a New Zealander and calling Auckland home is part of my story. Yet, there is so much I don't understand about Aotearoa. I ask questions, then listen. I study, read, visit.

And ask more questions and listen.

"The uninformed must improve their deficit, or die."

- THE CHESHIRE CAT

EPILOGUE

"I wonder if I shall fall right through the earth! How funny it'll seem to come out among the people that walk with their heads downwards! The Antipathies, I think—" (she was rather glad there was no one listening, this time, as it didn't sound at all the right word) "—but I shall have to ask them what the name of the country is, you know. Please, Ma'am, is this New Zealand or Australia?"

**- LEWIS CARROLL,
ALICE'S ADVENTURES IN WONDERLAND (1865)**

15 August 2021

While scrolling through my social media, an Etsy vendor's pair of owl earrings appeared on my feed. These looked like something my dear friend Athena would like. So I went to the Etsy shop, copied the link, and shared the earrings with her. Of course, she already was following this vendor and had the same owl, but in necklace form, saved in her cart. I browsed the rest of the items, spotting some intriguing rabbit necklaces. Then I noticed an Alice in Wonderland necklace - Alice, with her hands behind her back - a stance I often take, mirroring generations of Helms, looking up at the Cheshire cat.

In the last year, there have been more references to Alice in relation to me than ever before. I believe this is because I have a Cheshire cat, a British Shorthair, to be exact. Myla, our second British Shorthair, was adopted and became a member of our home in October 2020. Our first British Shorthair, Myrtle, was fourteen when she died in January 2020. When we put the deposit down on then Kinky Boots – the K litter name from the breeder, we were discussing names for our new kitten as we drove south to pick strawberries in Mount Vernon. I wanted to go with Marigold. Geoff hated that. Texting Athena that we decided to get the kitten, she told me that she had a dream last night– about Alice and her cat Dinah, and she just knew we were going to get our kitten. I toyed with naming our new cat Dinah but went with Myla for another bookish reason.

Seeing the necklace and loving it, I added it to my cart. However, I continued to feel like I couldn't get it just yet because I never actually read the book. I watched the Disney version when I was a kid, but I didn't know the story – the words on pages. I decided to get the unabridged audiobook from my library and listen to it on my Sunday walk.

Walking down the hill, I listened as Jim Dale read the story to me. I looked up with a start when Alice mentioned New Zealand. What?! What are the chances? Then how she questions who she is at the beginning of the book – I couldn't believe the connection to the moments I'd been wrestling with all year. As the story continued, I said to myself – *this is about colonization. Isn't it? I asked. I wonder if anyone has written about that. It seems so obvious.* I can't believe I never knew this and that this was the first time that I was "reading" the actual book.

As soon as I returned home from my walk, while guzzling water, I started an internet search [Alice's Adventure in Wonderland Colonization] – and I wasn't surprised that the search provided results. It seems there are two camps – those who believe Alice is the colonizer and others who see her as a member of Wonderland and, therefore, the one being colonized. However, the one character they all agree upon is the Queen of Hearts representing Queen Victoria. According to Amanda Bryan in her article "Alice's Struggle with Imperialism: Undermining the British Empire through Lewis Carroll's *Alice's Adventures in Wonderland*," the Queen comparison was embraced by Queen Victoria as noted in Stanley Weintraub's biography: "By taking a line spoken by the Queen of Hearts as her own, Queen Victoria not only recognises but seems to accept her resemblance to the Queen of Hearts." So it seems there is one point of agreement.

There are only two countries mentioned in Wonderland. Australia and New Zealand (the other side of the world from Britain). The Treaty for Waitangi was signed in 1840. Lewis Carroll, Charles Lutwidge Dodgson, wrote and published the book in 1865, a mere 25 years later, the length of my marriage. A lot happened in those 25 years: the Wairau incident, war in the north between the British and Māori led by Hōne Heke, New Zealand's first Parliament, Waikato chief Te Wherowhero became the first Māori King, the New Zealand Wars that continued until 1882, the Native Land Act, the New Zealand Settlements Act – which authorized the taking of land from Māori. What was Carroll/Dodgson hearing about Aotearoa New Zealand at the time? Delaney Krall, in the article "Why Lewis Carroll Disapproved of Imperialism," states:

> *The current events and culture surely influenced the writer's personality. . . His works,* Alice's Adventures in Wonderland, *suggests through certain scenes that he was not an advocate of imperialism during the Victorian era for reason that he disapproved of the invasiveness and*

imposition of culture because it caused chaos and confusion among the natives of the foreign lands.

Others, like Emma D. Graner, see Carroll's text as commentary on the travel narratives of the Victorian era. In her article "Dangerous Alice: Travel Narrative, Empire and *Alice's Adventures in Wonderland*," Graner states:

> *Alice poses a greater threat to Wonderland than Wonderland ultimately poses to her, and she makes good on this threat in the end. . . Carrol makes this underground world suggestive of the colonial landscape encountered by British travelers, and he renders Alice's adventures in similar conventional terms to those employed by writers of Victorian travel literature. In doing so, Carrol critiques the colonist discourse that undergirds the British imperial project as it manifested in the 1860s.*

A commentary on imperialism, colonization, settler colonization, and the narratives crafted and sold around the topic and at the expense of others. Clearly, others were seeing what I saw/heard as I listened to the story of Alice's adventures unfold.

However, the debate of whether Alice represents the colonizer or the colonized is one where I couldn't quite land on a conclusion. Most of the reading and research I found sat Alice firmly in the representation of Britain, British ideals. Alice takes on the role of a British subject in a new land. However, Amanda Bryan, citing and relying on research by M. Daphne Kutzer, states: "Alice, and a few other characters, can be seen as resembling the colonial 'other' in her relation to the authority figures in Wonderland, and the majority of the creatures of

Wonderland embody colonial attitudes about British subjects in its colonies." In this, Alice falls into the Queen's empire. All those seemingly colonizer actions translate instead to the struggle of not understanding the colonizer's culture and mores, and her own subversion to British rule.

I can't decide if I see Alice as the colonizer or the colonized. I see it both ways, which maybe speaks to some of the complexities of the settler colonizer. Her continual change of size alters her power dynamic throughout the story. At one point, she even suffers from her former "big" actions – when she fans herself back to smallness and finds herself swimming in a sea of her tears: "'I wish I hadn't cried so much!' said Alice, as she swam about trying to find her way out. 'I shall be punished for it now, I suppose, by being drowned in my own tears!'" Her movement in Wonderland meant she started to forget all the things she learned "(she was so much surprised, that for the moment she quite forgot how to speak good English)." But the duality wasn't new to Alice; it was in her nature to see herself as two people: "for this curious child was very fond of pretending to be two people." In the transnational life, in a way, Britain and Wonderland, Alice tries to understand and fit in, but at the same time, she influences things just by her being there, and she inserts herself into the lives of others. The March Hare, Dormouse, and Hatter all tell her there is no room at the tea party, but she says there is plenty and sits down. Under both areas of thought on Alice – this could be seen as the British arriving uninvited, or it could be seen the British telling the indigenous that there is no more room for them at the table/on the land. It is the Hare that states, "It wasn't very civil of you to sit down without being invited." It is later when the fundamental understanding of the table and party starts to make sense. Time doesn't change (a nod to the sun doesn't set on the British Empire, possibly) and those at the table move from one place to the next when the food (resources) are used up or no longer fulfilling them "'I want a clean cup,' interrupted the Hatter: 'let's all move one place on.' . . . The Hatter was the only one who got any advantage from the change: and Alice was a good deal worse off than before." In this case, Alice could be recognized as the colonized. Still, I'd argue she could also be the settler-colonizer with promises from the Crown of new land to discover, but who then realizes that the place was already occupied, and they are all left working through the consequences of the Empire's hand reaching out and taking another's land.

    I am not sure if I can fully argue Alice as settler-colonizer, but she is the one that traveled to Wonderland (not the other way around). While there, she dreamed of things from her old life: "'Nobody seems to like her, down here, and I'm sure she's the best cat in the world. Oh, my dear Dinah! I wonder if I shall ever see you any more.'" Her continual return to Dinah at the beginning of her time in Wonderland is a harkening back to the familiar. She remembers her other life in Wonderland while trying to navigate her new state of being. She compares this new place to her old home and her understanding of the culture she was raised in, yet she wants Wonderland to feel familiar and like home. She wants to belong. However, how does one belong in a place that belongs to others and is being controlled by an "off with her/his head" Queen detached (no pun intended) from her subjects and the lives they are trying to live far across the globe with different ways of thinking and vastly different cultures. Alice continues to ask who she is and struggles with her multiple selves.

    In a way, Alice struggles with belonging and not belonging, a space I am familiar with. I fully understand the two selves (warring inside her) in multiple ways – Becky/Rebecca and later United States of America/Aotearoa New Zealand. Alice has a cat as her guide, but it is always appearing and disappearing – a hint to spiritual gifts and the role of God/Spirit in my life. I'd say the most haunting aspect that resonates with me is the waking up in "home" and realizing the work of continuing to understand self and place remains. While seeing my own place/history in the destruction of other people's home/land, there is still a desire resting inside me to learn and return. To belong while always knowing belonging is impossible.

I bought the necklace.

"I'm a stranger. You're a stranger. Together we are . . . strangers."

– THE CHESHIRE CAT

WORKS CITED

Allen, Chadwick. *Blood Narrative: Indigenous Identity in American Indian and Maori Literary and Activist Texts.* Durham: Duke University Press, 2002. Print.

Bryan, Amanda. "Alice's Struggle in Imperialism: Undermining the British Empire through Lewis Carroll's *Alice's Adventures in Wonderland.*" Academia. 17 August 2021. https://www.academia.edu/10171193/Alices_Struggle_with_Imperialism_Undermining_the_British_Empire_through_Alices_Adventures_in_Wonderland

Buonomano, Dean. *Your Brain is a Time Machine: The Neuroscience and Physics of Time.* New York: W.W. Norton & Company, Inc., 2017, Print.

Buck, Peter. *The Coming of the Māori.* Christchurch: Whitcombe and Tombs LTD, 1970. Print.

Byrnes, Giselle. " 'Relic of 1840' or founding document? The treaty, the tribunal and concepts of time." *Kōtuitui: New Zealand Journal of Social Sciences Online.* 1:1 (2010): 1-12.

Carroll, Lewis. *Alice's Adventures in Wonderland.* Falkirk: Puffin Books, 2015. Print.

DeLoughrey, Elizabeth M. *Routes and Roots: Navigating Caribbean and Pacific Island Literatures.* Honolulu: University of Hawai'i Press, 2007. Print.

DeLoughrey, Elizabeth. "The Spiral Temporality of Patricia Grace's *Potiki*." *ARIEL: A Review of International English Literature*. 30.1 (1999): 59-83. Print.

Dyck, Cornelius J. *An Introduction to Mennonite History*. 3rd ed. Scottdale: Herald Press, 1993. Print.

Freud, Sigmund. "The 'Uncanny.'" *The Norton Anthology of Theory and Criticism*. 2nd ed. Ed. Vincent B Leitch. New York: W.W. Norton & Company, 2010. 824-841. Print.

Friesen, Wardlow. "The Demographic Transformation of Inner City Auckland." *New Zealand Population Review*. 35 (2009): 55-74. Print. 6 June 2021.

Goldberg, Myla. *Bee Season*. New York: Anchor Books, 2000. Print.

Gordon, Elizabeth. 'Speech and accent,' *Te Ara - the Encyclopedia of New Zealand,* http://www.TeAra.govt.nz/en/speech-and-accent (accessed 30 April 2021).

Graner, Emma D. "Dangerous Alice: Travel Narrative, Empire, and *Alice's Adventures in Wonderland*." *CEA Critic,* vol. 76 no. 3, 2014, p. 252-258. Project MUSE, doi:10.1353/cea.2014.0035. 15 Aug. 2021.

Grimshaw, Charlotte. *The Mirror Book*. Auckland: Vintage - Penguin Random House New Zealand, 2021. Print.

Hau'ofa, Epeli. *We are the Ocean*. Honolulu: University of Hawai'i Press, 2008. Print.

Himes, Mavis. *The Power of Names: Uncovering the Mystery of What we are Called*. Lanham: Rowman & Littlefield, 2016. Print.

Hunsicker, Ronald J. *Growing Up Gottshall*. Morgantown: Masthof Press, 2015. Print

Kisner, Jordan. *Thin Places: Essays from in Between*. New York: Picador, 2020. Print.

Krall, Delaney. "Why Lewis Carroll Disapproved of Imperialism." *Lamar Critical Edition*. 17 August 2021. https://down-the-rabbit-hole.weebly.com/why-lewis-carroll-disapproved-of-imperialism.html

Lanyadoo, Jessica. *Episode 196: Astrology Hot Take – The MC/10th House. Ghost of a Podcast*, 17 March 2021. Web. 13 June 2021.

Orange, Claudia. *The Treaty of Waitangi*. Wellington: Allen & Unwin New Zealand Limited, 1987. Print.

Racioppi, Jennifer. *Cosmic Health*. New York: Little Brown Spark, 2021. Print.

Somerville, Alice Te Punga. *Once Were Pacific: Māori Connections to Oceania*. Minneapolis: University of Minnesota Press, 2012. Print.

Tippett, Krista. *Serene Jones: On Grace. On Being*. Onbeing.org. The On Being Project, 5 Dec. 2019. Web. 15 July 2020.

Tippett, Krista. *Joy Harjo: The Whole of Time. On Being*. Onbeing.org. The On Being Project, 13 May 2021. Web. 13 May 2021.

Tyson, Lois. *Critical Theory Today*. New York: Garland Publishing, Inc, 1999. Print.

Weslager, C.A. *The Delaware Indians: A History*. New Brunswick: Rutgers University Press, 2008. Print.

Williams, Les R. Tumoana and Manuka Henare. "The Double Spiral and Ways of Knowing." *MAI Review*. 3.3 (2009). 6 June 2021.

ACKNOWLEDGMENTS

Thank you to Nick Courtright at Atmosphere Press for taking a chance on this unusual multimedia, hybrid-genre memoir. Thank you to Alex Kale for your guidance and Tammy Letherer for the wonderful editorial advice.

I am tremendously grateful to Kristiana Kahakauwila for her endless encouragement and support. Her guidance and chats over tea (or wine) were instrumental to the development of the core of this book. Special thanks to Brenda Miller for her wise, wizard-like ways with scissors and tape in the very early draft of this book. I can't imagine my writing life and journey without you, Tiana and Brenda. You are both so influential in my growth as a writer and scholar.

To the Graduate School at Western Washington University – thank you for awarding me the grant to assist in my research in Aotearoa New Zealand. It offered me the opportunity to return, twenty years later, to the beginning, to Waitangi, which set this project (and my life) on a trajectory I didn't expect.

My deepest thanks and appreciation to Rodney Baker for taking me on the most magical Aotearoa tiki tour, and for his careful review of "Do you have your camera?"

I am thankful to my parents for raising me in the Pennsylvania German community, which cultivated my tenacious work ethic and my love of a good story.

Many thanks to Colleen Lutz Clemens for your relentless support and encouragement. You are my lifeline when I spiral out of control. You are the person I run to when I want someone to rejoice with me in the magic of discovery. Thank you for reading many drafts of this book and for always being my voice of reason. You are a treasure.

Athena Roth, Frond, kindred spirit and sister in woo. You are pure magic, and this book wouldn't be entering out into the world without you. Thank you for ALWAYS being my cheerleader. I appreciate all you do to help me be a better person.

For reading and workshopping components of this manuscript at various stages of the process, I'd like to thank Dayna Kidd Patterson, Marley Simmons-Abril, Kathryn Kendall-Weed, Jenny Lara, Fallon Sullivan, Mike Oliphant, Rosemary Engelfried, Megan Spiegel, Suzanne Paola, Carol Guess, Theresa Warbuton, Christopher Loar, Bruce Beasly, Rob Rich, Julia Hands, Lindsay Petrie, Ellie Rogers, Cindy-Lou Holland-Rhodes, Jocelyn Marshall, Lydia Weiso, Eli Walker, Alyssa Quinn, Chloe Allmand, Karoline Schaufler, Tracy Haack, Christina Holt, Alissa Delafuente, Jenna Gernand, Sarah Appleton-Pine, Cindy Sherwin, and Becki Burgesser.

Thank you to the editors at STWP Literary Awards Program for the best compliment – "We loved the strange coolness of this manuscript" – You couldn't have said anything more perfect to this Aquarian Sun. In the words of Chris Corsini, *Aquarius, you are here to study the system, break that system and build a new one.*

I am indebted to Jessica Lanyadoo and her astrology lessons on *Ghost of a Podcast*. Thank you to Megan Havens for introducing me to the podcast.

Thank you to my friends and family who responded to my question about Becky Helm: Bonnie, Tracy, Jen, Amy, Lynn, Eileen, Susan, Nadine, Becky, Anne, Scott, David, Jessica, Stine,

Jen, Michele, Ninni, Nancy, Nancy, and Sherri.

Aroha nui to my family and friends in Aotearoa New Zealand. Reece, Renee, Jet, and Nova – thank you for always providing us a home to return to in Tāmaki Makaurau Auckland. Clive and Steph – thank you for the constant question of *When are you coming home?* as a reminder we are loved and missed. A special thanks to Renee Young-Beardsall for her willingness to find, purchase, and mail books for me.

In loving memory of Myrtle. Your support of my writing was constant. You never left my side through drafts, research, and revisions. I miss you.

Thank you to Dwayne for always being with me. I miss you.

Finally, to the person who is central to this whole collection, my lovely. Geoffrey, your unending support means the world to me. You have encouraged me time and again to discover myself and the world around me. Thank you for joining me on this journey.

ABOUT ATMOSPHERE PRESS

Atmosphere Press is an independent, full-service publisher for excellent books in all genres and for all audiences. Learn more about what we do at atmospherepress.com.

We encourage you to check out some of Atmosphere's latest releases, which are available at Amazon.com and via order from your local bookstore:

Finding Us, by Kristin Rehkamp

The Ideological and Political System of Banselism, by Royard Halmonet Vantion (Ancheng Wang)

Unconditional: Loving and Losing an Addict, by Lizzy and Adam

Telling Tales and Sharing Secrets, by Jackie Collins, Diana Kinared, and Sally Showalter

Nursing Homes: A Missionary's Journey Through Heaven's Waiting Room, by Tim Eatman Ph.D.

Timeline of Stars, by Joe Adcock

A Boy Who Loved Me, by Wilson Semitti

The Injustice in Justice, by Charmaine Loverin

Living in the Gray, by Katie Weber

Living with Veracity, Dying with Dignity, by Alison Clay-Duboff

Noah's Rejects, by Rob Kagan

A lot of Questions (with no answers)?, by Jordan Neben

Cowboy from Prague: An Immigrant's Pursuit of the American Dream, by Charles Ota Heller

Sleeping Under the Bridge, by Melissa Baker

The Only Prayer I Ever Have to Say Is Thank You, by M. Kaya Hill

Amygdala Blue, by Paul Lomax

A Caregiver's Love Story, by Nancie Wiseman Attwater

ABOUT THE AUTHOR

Rebecca Beardsall (MA, Lehigh University; MFA, Western Washington University) is the author of *My Place in the Spiral* and the co-editor of three books, including *Philadelphia Reflections: Stories from the Delaware to the Schuylkill*. Rebecca is the nonfiction editor at Minerva Rising Press.

She grew up in Quakertown, Pennsylvania, and has lived in various places, including Scotland, Canada, Montana, and Aotearoa/New Zealand. She currently resides in Bellingham, Washington, with her husband and cat.